MEANINGFUL GRADING

A GUIDE FOR FACULTY IN THE ARTS

ISBN:
Cloth 978-1-946684-48-6
Paper 978-1-946684-49-3
Ebook 978-1-946684-50-9

Library of Congress Cataloging-in-Publication Data
Names: Haugnes, Natasha, 1965- author. | Holmgren, Hoag, author. | Springborg, Martin,
    author.
Title: Meaningful grading : a guide for faculty in the arts / Natasha Haugnes, Hoag Holmgren,
    and Martin Springborg.
Description: First edition. | Morgantown : West Virginia University Press, 2018. | Includes
    bibliographical references.
Identifiers: LCCN 2018010255| ISBN 9781946684486 (cloth) | ISBN 9781946684493
    (pbk.) | ISBN 9781946684509 (ebook)
Subjects: LCSH: College students--Rating of. | Art students--Rating of. | Grading and
    marking (Students) | Arts--Study and teaching (Higher)--Evaluation.
Classification: LCC LB2368 .H38 2018 | DDC 371.27--dc23
LC record available at https://lccn.loc.gov/2018010255

Book and cover design by Than Saffel / WVU Press

MEANINGFUL GRADING

NATASHA HAUGNES, HOAG HOLMGREN, AND MARTIN SPRINGBORG

WEST VIRGINIA UNIVERSITY PRESS / MORGANTOWN 2018

For my family at home, my family at the Academy of Art University, my family in the POD Network, and the family I still have yet to meet.

—NH

For my ever-inspiring troupe: Leda, Soren, Anders, Mirabelle.

—HH

For the family I've chosen, and continue to choose. You are loved.

—MS

RESPONSIBLE TEACHING is an all-out effort. Only a maximum of patience, imagination, and zeal can make an effective case to students for caring. The best of them always want more than just facts; they want to see an example of how to live with the facts, and perhaps even by them.

Robert Adams, *Why People Photograph*, 1994

CONTENTS

Part II: During the Semester

Communicating Goals

Emphasizing Process over Results

CONTENTS *continues on next page*

CONTENTS *continued*

Part II: During the Semester *continued*

Teaching Content and Skills

Rubrics

The Critique

Part III: Post-semester

FIGURE 1. *BEAR (MEADOW)* BY GARY HAWKINS, WARREN WILSON COLLEGE, NC

Introduction

Meaningful Grading: A Guide for Faculty in the Arts is written for post-secondary arts instructors in all stages of their careers. This includes but is not limited to faculty in design, architecture, fine and visual arts, media arts, literary arts, printmaking, and performance arts. The book addresses issues of perennial importance to first-time instructors and offers new perspectives to more experienced instructors looking to refresh their teaching. Department chairs and deans who are adapting to a changing landscape of accountability will also find this book useful as a resource for effective practices. Finally, instructors who may be well-versed in teaching other disciplines but new to instruction in the arts can glean ideas for transferring their practices to new creative fields.

The contents are written in tip form and arranged to mirror the flow of an academic semester, so that information can be located and implemented quickly and easily. We examine a broad range of topics through the lens of grading, feedback, and assessment, addressing many of the recurring challenges for faculty in the arts. For the purposes of this book, grading refers to the assignment of a quantitative score, a number or a letter, to some aspect of student performance. Feedback consists of qualitative comments on some aspect of student performance. Assessment embodies grading, feedback, and all other ways that instructors evaluate teaching and learning in the classroom. We believe that clear and accurate grading, feedback, and assessment are essential aspects of effective teaching in all disciplines. However, these practices often pose unique challenges in the arts.

Strong teaching requires careful planning, even though the time constraints of academe do not always allow for it. This book is designed so that each tip can stand alone, offering concise, pedagogically sound direction for the busy faculty member. Anyone with five minutes can find a tip or technique to implement half an hour later in the classroom or studio. Faculty with a deeper interest in a topic can choose to read a series of tips or delve into some of the resources suggested in the further reading sections.

These are the three main questions that drive *Meaningful Grading*:

► How can faculty in the arts grade student work in ways that improve learning and support artistic development?

► What does effective grading in the arts look like?

► How can faculty in the arts develop and improve their teaching and grading over the course of their careers?

The path of the artist and the path of the educator often converge. One example of this common ground is the imperative to grow and evolve. Ongoing renewal requires an awareness of the tendencies to become complacent and to plateau professionally or aesthetically, without exploring possibilities for fresh engagement and new development. And it requires a willingness and ability to resist these tendencies.

Embracing and committing to process can help. Much of the work we do as instructors in the arts is to nurture process. We create and hold a space where students do the work, where goals are articulated and achieved together, and where feedback and assessment encourage an organic unfolding. In doing so, we acquire a kind of resilience in the face of culturally sanctioned habits and narratives that seek to limit or over-simplify the ways we instruct and the ways our students develop as artists. As we embrace process, it becomes increasingly clear that there is no foolproof recipe or best approach, for either artist-in-progress or instructor. We can thus see our instructional work as a project that benefits from ongoing revision.

We offer this book as an invitation to join or recommit to a longstanding dialogue between art and critical thinking. Plato famously banned poetry and other arts from his ideal republic where philosophy was to be privileged over all other modes of inquiry and expression. Perhaps Plato suspected that "Art is dangerous, in that it challenges reason's suprem-acy."[1] These two forces—the creative and generative on one hand, and the analytical and rational on the other—must somehow function in our courses in a mutually beneficial way if we are serious about support-ing and assessing student learning and artistic development. It is our hope that this book provides some practical resources to help instruc-tors in the arts keep the dialogue alive and vital.

FIGURE 2. *BOOK 2 (FROM A COLLABORATION BETWEEN JAPAN AND THE UNITED STATES OF AMERICA)* BY RURIKO MIYAMOTO AND KATHERINE SANDNAS, HIBBING COMMUNITY COLLEGE, MN

PART I

Course Design and Preparation

Part one is designed to help you prepare for teaching, ideally before the start of the semester.

Examining Your Own Beliefs and Biases

Faculty artists come to the profession of teaching with underlying beliefs and knowledge about teaching and learning. Understanding your own perspective can help you create and implement effective grading and assessment practices.

Knowing Your Context

How does your own institution define success? What is the grading and assessment culture of your institution and department? What are the student learning goals for your institution and department? Answering questions like these can define and clarify the parameters within which you are working and help illuminate best practices.

Defining Success in Your Course

Defining what the big markers of success will look like in your course ahead of time helps you design the grading and assessment into your course from the outset. Integrating the assessment in this way ensures that grading supports teaching and learning—that it is not tacked on as an afterthought.

FIGURE 3. *JELLYFISH TREND BOARD FOR FASHION* BY AIMEE BINH YEN TRUONG, ACADEMY OF ART UNIVERSITY, CA

Tip 1

_____

Quantifying the Qualitative

How can I grade art? It's subjective. How can I attach a number to the quality of concept, aesthetics, or craftsmanship? These are central questions that many thoughtful faculty artists ask.

On the surface, it does seem paradoxical to attempt to quantify art when art is often precisely that which defies definition and breaks rules. On the other hand, if we are teaching art, we must believe that it can be learned. And if students can progress in that learning, we must find a way to describe their progress—to quantify it.

Faculty artists often speak wistfully of the instructors in math or science departments who *have it so easy* when it comes to counting things that their students do and proving that learning outcomes are being met. Math and science teachers may be more comfortable with the spreadsheets and numbers they use to calculate grades, but when it comes to quantifying *learning*, no department has it figured out perfectly. Anyone who says they do is probably missing something important.

Here are a few guidelines to bear in mind as you develop a quantifiable assessment system for students' work:

▶ Remember that your system will not be perfect. Artistic ability and growth, like most abilities, cannot be measured perfectly. There will be holes in the grading systems. There will be aspects of the art that you never even talk about with the students. That is okay. You will likely continue to revise your grading system throughout your career.

▶ Focus on one course at a time. Courses have different goals or outcomes, so you need to develop distinct grading systems for each one that you teach. For example, a beginning design course may focus on developing skills for seeing and selecting color palettes for existing designs, while a more advanced course emphasizes using those skills in combination with composition, layout, or even market research skills. The first course's grading system will likely focus on smaller, more discrete units of learning, while the second course's system may de-emphasize the discrete skills in favor of integrated skills.

▶ Start with the "big buckets." Gather a range of student work for a particular course from previous semesters. Divide the work into three piles: not passing, passing, and high passing. As you describe each pile of work, you will begin to establish the baseline expectations of quality for this project or course. Avoid getting too granular— don't focus on the distinction between A- and B+, for example—at this point. Once you determine the expectations for these initial categories, the more refined grades will fall into place more easily.

▶ Don't ignore process. As you go through the "big buckets" exercise described above, you may find that one piece does not look as good as the others, but you know the student who created the piece made remarkable progress over the course of a semester. If progress is an aspect of performance that is central to your course, define what that progress looks like. It may entail elements such as the amount of engagement in critique, questions the student asked, or how many revisions or iterations the student completed between critiques.

▶ Don't try to quantify the rare, inexplicably wonderful artistic moments that occur. Or at least, don't begin there. Many instructors, when asked about their students' work, want to talk about the truly exceptional pieces from the truly exceptional students. Many faculty artists have expressions to describe this *je ne sais quoi*, wow factor, or thing that makes it soar. Moments of exceptional sensitivity, talent, or insight are exciting and should be celebrated (perhaps with a ceremonial rubric burning). And yes, it is difficult to quantify these moments. So don't.

FIGURE 4. *STARLINGS* BY SARAH BARSNESS, SOLANO COMMUNITY COLLEGE, CA

Tip 2

_____

Examining Aesthetic Sensibility

Investigating and clarifying our aesthetic tastes before the semester begins can help weed out unintentional or excessive bias when it comes time to grade or give feedback. If we're not careful, our comments about the value, or lack thereof, of well-known artists or art traditions can tempt students into creating work solely to please us. By extension, our choices of work that we present and discuss can perpetuate—or challenge—cultural values and assumptions in the classroom. We're entitled to articulate personal opinions about art, but we need to be mindful about the impact of sharing and unpacking opinions in the classroom.

In this self-examination process, we anticipate and identify the unintended messages we send about the aesthetics we value and our opinions about art. These messages can be detrimental to fostering a learning environment and a genuine development process. How can we support students in developing unique work and opinions independent of our own? Consider the following ways to engage in this investigative process:

- Reflect on the following questions:

  - What message about aesthetic values am I sending when I share my opinions about art?

  - When I express an opinion, am I being clear that I am expressing an opinion?

  - Am I sending an unintended message by omitting certain artists or art movements from the course or from the discussion?

  - Am I able to talk about interesting or instructive qualities of a work of art that I personally dislike?

  - Does my own aesthetic bias influence my grading, or am I sending the message that it might?

- Build activities into your class where you discuss the contributions of different traditions and schools in order to facilitate a creative, open, and dynamic environment.

- Include discussions about contributions by artists from nondominant cultures.

- Identify art that represents a wide variety of styles, including some that you respect but don't necessarily *like,* to share with students as examples for discussion throughout the semester.

- Resist the temptation to use your own work as an exemplar of excellence. Be clear that you do not use your own art because you don't want students to be tempted to mimic your work.

- Include an explicit policy in your syllabus about expectations regarding styles and genres. For example, if your course emphasizes a particular style of drawing or genre of film, make that clear.

- Use a rubric for grading (see tips 35–40).

- Model examples of constructive feedback that get beyond personal taste and focus instead on specific aspects of the work. Have students distinguish between personal reactions such as "I don't like nature photography" or "I don't like poetry that rhymes," and more observational, analytical, and constructive comments such as "The long tree shadows in this photo create a sense of stillness." Discuss which types of comments are more helpful when discussing peer work.

Tip 3

The Apprenticeship of Observation

Whether we are aware of it or not, we have learned a tremendous amount about teaching from simply watching our own teachers. And these lessons stick with us—for better, or in some cases, for worse. Dan Lortie calls this informal process the *apprenticeship of observation*.[2]

Whether we emulate the techniques of instructors who inspired us or replicate ineffective teaching practices, we are likely unaware of why we're doing it, according to the apprenticeship of observation model. Sometimes those teaching practices contradict our current teaching beliefs. For example, you might *believe* that students' progress is best assessed through their projects, but in practice you base your grades on exams because that is how your own instructors assessed you. Even when we emulate effective teaching, exploring the underlying scholarship supporting those teaching methods will strengthen our practices and deepen our beliefs.

Recognizing our inclination to teach the way we were taught is the first step to breaking out of ineffective patterns of instruction, strengthening effective ones, and seeking out opportunities to make improvements. In order to align our teaching and grading with our beliefs, we need to recognize how our teaching and grading practices have been influenced through our own apprenticeship of observation. How to do that, and where to take the first steps are the key challenges. If you are on a campus with a teaching center, that is an excellent place to start. But even if you do not have access to a teaching center, the following ideas can help you examine the connection between underlying beliefs and teaching habits. Most of these have to do with observation—either inviting peers to observe you or observing the successful teaching practices at your institution:

▸ Schedule classroom observations with someone you trust. (Most teaching center observations are completely confidential, between you and the teaching center staff.) It's easy to feel vulnerable being observed and instinctively shut down to the idea of staff or even fellow faculty entering your classrooms. Moving past this initial feeling will lead to positive connections and explorations of teaching that will likely yield positive outcomes in your classrooms.

▸ Attend workshops on teaching and learning practices. Your own teaching center may offer these. There are also excellent conferences and webinars on teaching that are available through other colleges or organizations.

▸ Schedule time to discuss teaching practices, along with underlying assumptions and beliefs, with one or more of your department colleagues, even if it's just over coffee.

▸ Connect with faculty from *other* departments around teaching and learning issues to gain exposure to teaching methods not employed in your own discipline. Sometimes these types of meetings are arranged through teaching centers as well—whether within departments or across departments.

▶ Take the knowledge that you gain through the above personal connections and pursue readings on topics most relevant to your own teaching practice. Teaching center staff and peers will be able to help with reading lists, and there are many excellent articles and ideas on websites associated with teaching centers at other colleges.

Tip 4

Novices and Experts

"I'm not going to tell you exactly what to do. Trust your gut!"

Comments such as these can be frustrating for beginning-level students. The instructor is asking the students to approach a challenge with more sophistication than they possess. And those same instructors may become frustrated by students who want step-by-step solutions spoon-fed to them after they have received less than satisfactory grades. This communication gap is common among people with vastly different levels of expertise, and it can interfere with clear communication and trust, both of which are crucial to grading and feedback.

Many who teach art are experts in their fields. According to theories about this expert-novice continuum,[3] experts have internalized so much of the content of their fields that they are able to immediately *see* or *feel* the entirety of a situation, and decisions throughout the creative process feel more intuitive than deliberate and step-by-step. The problem with becoming an expert is that once we are able to see and feel things in a certain way, it becomes almost impossible to remember what it was like *not* to see or feel them in that way. It can be difficult for an expert artist to give grades and feedback that take into account the challenges, assumptions, and frustrations a student may be experiencing. A mere awareness of the expert-novice dynamic can give instructors more patience with students, even if they do not remember what it was like to learn their craft.

There is no simple formula to becoming an expert, but one thing that many experts have in common is that they have usually engaged in 10,000 hours or ten years of focused, deliberate practice.[4] Deliberate practice consists of setting a specific goal, focusing on the task, getting and incorporating informed immediate feedback, and repeating the task until one meets the goal. Instructors can bridge the expert-novice gap while guiding students toward becoming experts in the following ways:

▸ Present grades and comments in a way that illuminates a way forward, encouraging process and artistic evolution. Focus comments on the rationale behind the letter grades that you've assigned to student work.

▸ Be aware of when you are asking novice students to solve expert-level problems. Consider simplifying the projects. Or "scaffold" complex projects so that they are more achievable for novice students. (See tip 13.)

▸ Understand that novice students often lack the vocabulary to explain what they see. Be explicit in your teaching of vocabulary to support their increasingly complex understandings.

▶ Continue to ask questions such as "What is your gut reaction?" when you have students look at unfamiliar work, but do not expect their gut reactions to be as sophisticated as your own. Have students assess their own development as they answer that question at the beginning of a semester and again at the end of a semester. Their answers will reveal their changing ways of looking at work. It may not progress in a linear way. Often, when going through a particularly disruptive period of learning, students reorganize their thinking and feel that they are going backwards. Talk to students about this process.

▶ Have students analyze and reflect on the quality of the time they are spending on homework, studio time, and work done away from class. How much of the total time was actually deliberate and focused practice? What does deliberate, focused practice feel like? What does easy busywork feel like? What does work that is too difficult feel like?

▶ Invite students to discuss the grades and comments you give. What kinds of comments do they find useful? What do they find less useful? Analyze their answers and adjust your feedback to their level accordingly.

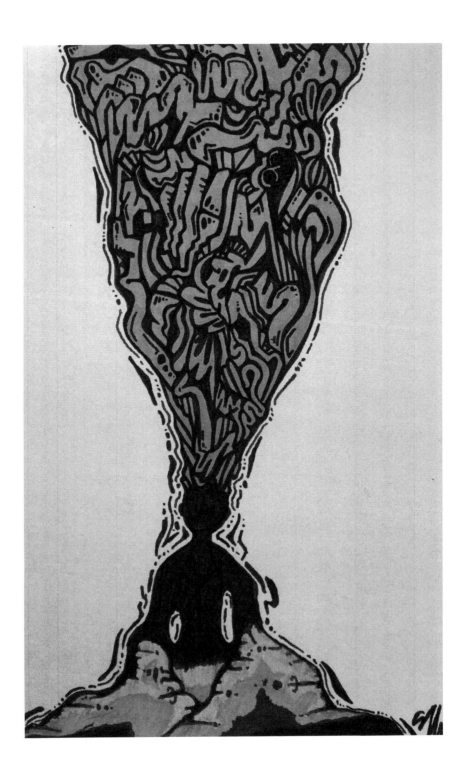

Tip 5

Getting Involved

Teaching at an institution of higher education can be a solitary experience, especially for part-time faculty or faculty just beginning their
careers. Either you teach courses at odd times of the day, when very few of
your colleagues are around, or you are so swamped with your teaching
responsibilities that you have little time for anything else. After a year or
more of this, it's easy to resign yourself to working in your own silo within
a much larger college or university. But it's important to break out of this
mode of thinking and to become involved outside of your own immediate
area, focus, discipline, or slate of courses.

Getting involved more broadly at your college or university has many
benefits. Most immediately, it will help you to become part of a community of educators. This connection to the larger community often leads to
trusting relationships with other educators. As those relationships build,
you gain a better sense of how your teaching efforts align with those of
other faculty and departments. This can help you in designing your
courses and assessing and grading student work, with an eye toward
student success not only in your disciplinary area(s) but also in the
broader college or university. Being knowledgeable about institutional

FIGURE 5 (OPPOSITE). *UNTITLED* BY SOREN HOLMGREN, NAROPA UNIVERSITY, CO

mission, goals, and initiatives can help you align your teaching with your department and institution, creating a more cohesive experience for students.

If you are seeking promotion or tenure, becoming connected to institutional mission and values—paired with meeting your faculty colleagues outside of your own discipline and serving with them on committees—can never hurt, especially if your institution's review process includes service. And if you are working as part-time faculty, taking these steps can sometimes improve your chances of filling a full-time appointment down the road—either at your current institution or another.

So how do you become involved? What steps should you take, and what are the most logical points of entry? Leora Baron-Nixon, in her book *Connecting Non Full-Time Faculty to Institutional Mission*, lists other ways that faculty can get involved at their institutions—including but not limited to representing departmental or college-wide issues on the faculty senate and participating open forums.[5]

Keep your ear to the ground, read some of those all-staff emails, and consider one or more of the following:

▶ Seek out your institution's professional development staff and committees, and see where you can contribute and how you can benefit from involvement.

▶ Plan to attend meetings in your department, cross-departmental gatherings that may interest you, or other events where your knowledge and expertise may be valued.

- Ask to be included in portfolio reviews or on juries for exhibits in your department or larger institution. The discussions that take place on those committees can give you a sense of what quality of work your department expects.

- Participate in the larger life of your institution (joining departmental or area-specific clubs, planning campus events such as guest speakers or conferences, etc.).

- Finally, consider getting involved in your institution's or your department's accreditation or reaccreditation efforts. For example, offer to serve on a task force related to writing your college's or university's portfolio or application for regional accreditation or reaccreditation. Related to that experience, you may also be interested in serving as a reviewer for such regional accrediting bodies. They are often looking for faculty and staff who are interested in serving this way, and this experience will be helpful as you volunteer in this process within your own department or at your institution.

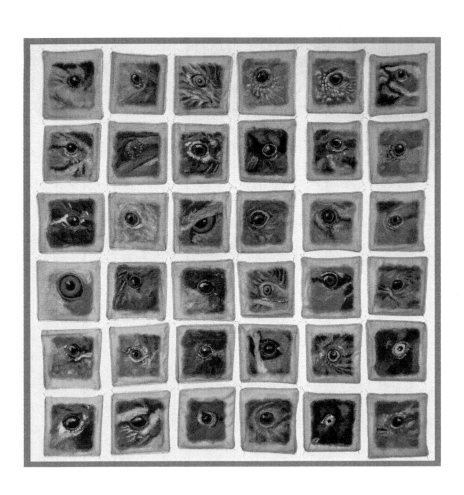

FIGURE 6. *BIRDS' EYE VIEW* BY SARAH BARSNESS, SOLANO COMMUNITY COLLEGE, CA

Tip 6

Implications of Grades

Grades are a form of communication to students about their performance relative to a specific set of criteria or expectations in a course. In our individual classrooms, grades should be symbolic of an intricate but clear web of criteria and expectations, but they are really only a shorthand notation of those expectations, and they make up only part of our communication with students. Grades should be accurate, of course, but to the student, they likely do not mean a whole lot outside of the context of the rich critiques, conversations, rubrics, and feedback that are woven into the class. When communicating with a student in the context of a course, for example, you have the ability to distinguish between a C that is earned for hard work and inconsistent outcomes, and a C that is earned for strong final work and inconsistent process.

Grades also communicate students' progress to other offices and departments at the institution. And these entities rely exclusively on grades to make determinations about students' academic fates. Institutions rely on accurate grades from you to maintain the integrity of their programs, and in some cases, to comply with federal regulations. In the United States, for example:

▸ Enrollment advisors use course grades to determine the courses in which students are eligible to enroll. For example, a D or F in Design Principles 1 will likely prevent a student from enrolling in Design Principles 2.

▸ Academic probation or academic dismissal policies rely on grades to determine whether students are eligible to continue with their studies, and under what circumstances. Students on academic probation may be required to attend special tutoring or to enroll in a study skills course, for example.

▸ The US Department of Homeland Security gathers reports on grades and attendance records of international students. Failing grades or low GPAs can put a student at risk of being sent back to their country of origin.

▸ Financial aid of many types, both government-sponsored and private, is also dependent on students' maintaining specific GPAs.

▸ Athletic team eligibility typically has a minimum academic performance level requirement. Students who do not meet minimum academic performance levels may be cut from a team and lose their athletic scholarships.

▸ Honor rolls and deans' lists are determined by GPAs.

Instructors are not necessarily responsible for knowing all of these specific thresholds, which vary widely among countries, states, institutions, and even departments within an institution. We are, however, responsible for making sure that our grading is meaningful and transparent, not just to us, but to our department directors and other university officials who may question our grades for a particular student. Grading honestly and accurately within our courses ensures that others can maintain the integrity of our institutions and appropriately guide students' enrollment.

Tip 7

Course Design: An Overview

Why discuss course design in a book about grading? Because grading, if it is to be meaningful to students, must be intentionally integrated into the whole course. Whether you are designing a course from scratch or trying to understand a course that you have been assigned to teach, it is crucial to understand how the following three components of a course work together to support learning.

GOALS: How will your students be different at the end of the course? What will they know? What beliefs will have changed? How do these goals differ from and align with other courses in your program? Goals are the destination for students' learning in your course. They should be articulated in ways that are measurable and concrete (as course-level student learning outcomes) so that both you and your students know when they have been met.

TEACHING AND LEARNING ACTIVITIES: What will your students do in and out of class? What will you do to support them in meeting the goals you have shared with them? Teaching and learning activities include all of the things that happen within the confines of the course: lectures, critiques, demos, homework assignments, practice exercises, major projects, field trips, readings, videos, and course discussions.

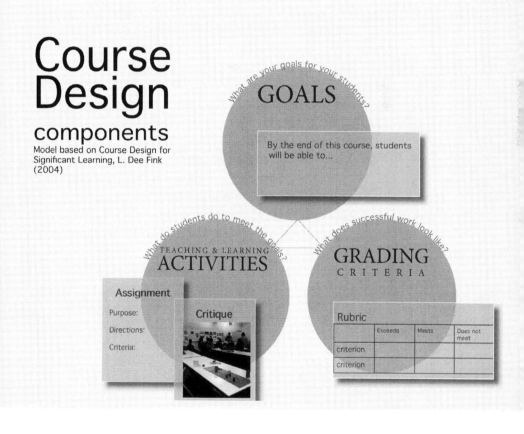

Course Design
components

Model based on Course Design for
Significant Learning, L. Dee Fink
(2004)

What are your goals for your students?

GOALS

By the end of this course, students
will be able to...

What do students do to meet the goals?

TEACHING & LEARNING
ACTIVITIES

What does successful work look like?

GRADING
CRITERIA

Assignment

Purpose:

Directions:

Criteria:

Critique

Rubric

	Exceeds	Meets	Does not meet
criterion			
criterion			

FIGURE 7. *COURSE DESIGN COMPONENTS BASED ON L. DEE FINK'S "CREATING SIGNIFICANT LEARNING EXPERIENCES"* BY NATASHA HAUGNES

Some are very focused, and others are broad; some take fifteen minutes of class time, while others take many hours over several weeks. The activities are all of the dots on the map that is your syllabus.

ASSESSMENT: What does success in this particular class look like? Assessment is the criteria, and by extension the grading and feedback systems that you set up, to determine whether teaching and learning have been successful and whether the student is ready for the next level of the program. At the very minimum, an instructor should be able to articulate assessment criteria by completing the following sentence: I know students have met the goals when they [do ____ in the final assignment], or [behave in a particular way], or [approach a problem in a particular way]. When I see that a student [does the opposite], I know he or she has not met the goals of the course and might need to repeat it.

The backward course design process suggests starting with the goal, envisioning evidence of success (main assignments and assessment criteria), and then planning the teaching and learning activities to guide students to the learning goals and production of evidence.

But one can enter this process at any of the three points. Sometimes, envisioning major projects or other learning activities is a more concrete entry point. And still other times, picturing successful and unsuccessful work in order to drill down to the assessment criteria is the best way to focus and define a course.

The course design process is iterative. Whichever of these three points serves as your entry, you will cycle through all the legs of the tripod multiple times throughout the course design process, adjusting and refining until each leg is in alignment to support deep learning. A web design instructor who starts with the activities may follow a line of thinking along these lines:

> I envision this course with lots of engaging critique of websites that students build. But what does a good critique (and website, for that matter) look like for this freshman level course? Students need to be able to recognize strong graphic layout and basic user experience (*goals*). I'll need to develop and present guidelines for what these goals look like at this level (*teaching activity*). I'll have them apply the guidelines to existing websites first (*learning activity*). Those guidelines will also be the basis for how I grade their websites (*assessment*). And we will need to do some training on constructive critique (*teaching and learning activity*). Maybe I should start giving feedback on the critiques according to constructive critique tips we discuss (*assessment*). I would love for them to get better at critiquing—I suppose constructive critique is a goal of the course as well (*goal*).

This type of iteration tightens a course by integrating the goals, activities, and assessment.

To get started on designing a course, revamping a course, or understanding a course that you have been given to teach, experiment with the following entry points and use the questions to guide you through designing—or understanding—your course:

▸   Define your goals. What are the goals? Do the activities guide students to the goals? How do you know that the goals have been met?

► Define the activities. What are the most important learning activities that the students do in the course? What does success (or non-success) look like for those activities? What are the goals reflected in these activities and criteria?

► Define your assessment criteria. What does it look like when students don't pass this course? What does it look like when they do pass? Which activities and assignments do you apply these assessment criteria to? What are the underlying goals toward which you guide students?

Tip 8

Course Design: Defining Goals

"But, I didn't know I was supposed to do that."

So goes the beginning of the dreaded I-don't-understand-why-you-can't-change-my-grade conversation. Most of us have had this frustrating discussion with students. We think we've articulated course goals and expectations clearly. Why should there be any misunderstanding? The solution: develop goals that are concrete and measurable, and make sure that you communicate them clearly to students.

Your course syllabus should clearly state the student learning outcomes (SLOs) for your course. An SLO is a specific, measurable, concrete learning goal for a course. It is always about what the *students* will do, not what you will do. SLOs should be written so that both you and your students know when they have been met. There are usually between four and eight per course. They usually start with the phrase: *by the end of this course, students will be able to* . . . Often, SLOs are already in existence for courses that you teach. But if you are creating your own course, put some thought into converting your goals into measurable, specific SLOs with the above opening. See the following examples:

GENERAL GOAL: Students will understand color theory. (Understanding can mean many things. One could dedicate their entire life to understanding color theory and never feel that they have mastered the concept.)

SLO: By the end of the course, students will be able to analyze and describe the value, hue, and saturation of colors in various works. (This is a much more specific, worthwhile endeavor that will push students further along the path to understanding color theory. You will be able to more easily teach to the SLO and assess when students have met it.)

GENERAL GOAL: Students will develop an appreciation for the great early photographers.

SLO: Students will be able to describe and explain the importance of early photographers' contributions to the field.

Tie the SLOs to assignment-level learning outcomes later. These links should always be transparent, so students can clearly see the importance of each assignment or action as a stepping-stone to the ultimate SLO. Students will be far more engaged in each learning opportunity if they understand how it fits overall within the course.

While assignments should be tied to overarching learning outcomes and course goals, there is no need to get overly detailed in your description of them in your syllabi. Doing so could actually be counterproductive, as you may want to make slight changes to assignments later in the course. Instead, give students a general overview of the types of assignments or learning opportunities they will be working on during the semester, and mention how these assignments will be weighted in the overall grading scheme. Save further assignment details, as well as assignment objectives, for the actual assignment outlines or descriptions you distribute during the semester.

Here are a few tips for defining and communicating the goals of your course:

▸ Create a section in your syllabus dedicated to stating and explaining student learning outcomes. Take SLOs directly from course descriptions on file at your institution, or create them according to the guidelines in this tip.

▸ Consider numbering the SLOs and using those numbers when assignments are listed in the syllabus and given later in the semester. This will give students a clear idea of which outcomes each assignment satisfies.

▸ Pay special attention to reviewing SLOs and expectations on the first day of class or at the beginning of the semester. Allow time for student questions, especially pertaining to your expectations of them.

FIGURE 8. *UNTITLED* BY ROBIN ESCHNER

Tip 9

Course Design: Teaching and Learning Activities

When writing a syllabus, instructors often begin with a list of all of the topics they want to cover. This is natural. We are excited about our disciplines, and many of us are motivated to teach because we want to share that passion and invite others in. So by all means, make that list—make it exhaustive! But then put it aside and list what your *students* will do. This list of student learning activities will create the backbone for your syllabus.

Start by identifying the anchor learning activities that your students will engage in: the signature projects or activities that set your course apart from others in the program. For example, in an introductory fashion sketching course, one of the main projects might be sketches of a collection based on a specific era's trends.

Then address the question: What information and skills do students need in order to complete these activities successfully? Carefully consider which things on your initial topics-to-cover list are most important and when they should be taught. For the fashion example above, students need basic knowledge of the era on which they are basing their collection and basic sketching skills. To prepare the students for this project, the instructor might plan the following teaching and learning activities: a series of short lectures on historical components, short quizzes to check comprehension, a series of demos and practice activities to build students' sketching skills, and discussions to help students begin to recognize historical influences in current collections.

Sequencing all your activities, demos, and critiques is an art in itself. There is no one correct way to do it. The manner in which you set up these activities should reflect your beliefs about how learning works, and also a sensitivity to the pacing of a course. It is likely to change as your own understanding evolves, or as your student population changes. So don't worry about getting it exactly right the first time, but be aware of when it works well—and when it doesn't—to build your underlying understanding.

Instructors who build their courses based solely on a list of things to cover are often at a loss as to how to assess student learning. These instructors often default to quizzes and exams to test how well students remember what was presented—to audit the learning.[6] While this model of teaching and learning is familiar to many of us from our own days as students, it generally does not promote deep learning, especially in fields of art and design. Focusing on learning activities keeps the focus on student growth. Teaching activities should always be in service of that student growth.

As you plan the learning activities in your course:

▸ Be explicit about the purpose of all of your teaching activities—all of your demos or lectures—and all of the learning activities. The purpose may be glaringly obvious to you, but not to your students. Explain what skills or knowledge each activity is about and why that knowledge is important in the larger picture of your course and discipline. This type of transparency can have a strong effect on keeping students engaged in their programs of study and bridge the novice-expert gap that usually exists between an instructor and students.[7]

▸ Consider beginning and ending your course with the same learning activity or a reflection on early work so that you and your students can see their growth over the course of a semester. For example, a comparison of sketches in week one and week fourteen can provide a satisfying illustration of learning in a basic drawing class.

▸ In foundations or skills-building courses that do not use anchor projects but instead many smaller skill-building assignments, consider having students create a mini-portfolio of work from the whole semester to demonstrate their growth. In courses focused on developing disciplinary ways of seeing or looking, consider a weekly journal to show their growth in thinking.

▸ Include short comprehension check activities to ensure that students are building the knowledge they need to complete a more comprehensive project. A comprehension check might take the form of a short quiz on some lecture or demo topic, or it could be a more informal classroom assessment technique[8] such as a one-minute paper in which students write the most important thing that they learned at the end of a short lecture.

▶ Consider the types of thinking, effort, and time you want students to engage in, and create your learning activities to elicit that. For example, a writing instructor who knew that revision is a crucial habit for writers was disappointed—semester after semester—that very few of her students ever resubmitted their work, despite her strong encouragement to do so. Finally, when she made revisions into required assignments, her students began spending a much higher proportion of their homework time revising their work.

▶ Vary the learning activities. Include focused practice activities as well as larger contextualized practice. Include writing as well as drawing and discussion. Plan individual, pair, and group work.

Tip 10

Course Design: Assessment Criteria

How do I decide if a student should pass my course? How will I explain my decision to that student who worked hard but earned a D?

Transparent criteria aid communication about grading, and they also help instructors focus their teaching and courses. To define these criteria, envision the evidence that you would present if your final grade were called into question—by your director, another instructor, the student, or in the form of an official institution-level appeal. Don't worry so much at first about the distinction between a B and a B-. Think instead about the distinction between passing (i.e., not outstanding, but sufficient) and not passing (i.e., complete, but not up-to-standard) work.

Narrow the evidence down to the most central pieces—the anchor projects or performances. For each central piece or component, answer the questions: What does this look like when a student has met the learning outcomes? What does it look like when a student has not met the learning outcomes? Your answers to these questions may be transformed into a rubric, or they may become a simple list of passing and not passing criteria. There are a number of main types of evidence and criteria you might identify:

▸ A final cumulative project where students display their learning for the semester. The criteria for passing the course are mostly reflected in the criteria for that project.

▸ Two or three main projects that reflect different aspects of learning from the semester.

▸ A portfolio or journal with a final entry or reflective piece that assesses the observable change throughout the course.

▸ A semester-long record of the students' contributions to discussion. A well-designed discussion rubric can provide transparent expectations and a clear record of students' contributions to discussion.

Once you have defined your baseline expectations for the course and have a clear idea of what the most important work looks like (or better yet, samples of student work), you have planted the goalposts for your semester. You and your students know what to aim for, and you can refer back to those baseline expectations should you ever need to discuss a grade with a student. These clearly defined expectations can also be helpful in case a grade is ever formally challenged.

These course-level criteria are also useful when you need to consider alternate paths for students to meet the goals of the course. For example, when working with a student with dyslexia, consider: Is it important that the final reflection be in a written format, or could it be an audio recording and still meet the criteria that reflect the core expectations of your course? Can the veteran with PTSD complete the movie poster final assignment for something other than *Apocalypse Now*?

FIGURE 9. *OLIVE OIL LABEL* BY NATASHA HAUGNES, ACADEMY OF ART UNIVERSITY, CA

Tip 11

Your Grading System: Math Matters

An instructor asked a colleague, "How much of the grade does the final project count for?"

"Oh, a lot," replied the colleague, "It is worth 100 points."

This answer made perfect sense to the instructor who said it. But out of context, it is meaningless. Just as the value of 100 is different when attached to dollars, euros, or ryals, the value of 100 points varies according to the proportion of possible points it represents. One hundred out of a total 200 possible points over the semester accounts for 50% of the grade, but 100 out of a possible 750 points accounts for 13.3%.

Math matters when setting up a point-based grading system. Once you have put careful effort into making visible what you value, you need to ensure that the final relative values of the components of your course are correctly weighted. Mistakes in setting up the system can result in inaccurate grades, even for well-intentioned instructors. For example, an instructor who began grading student discussions figured out partway through the semester that students could pass the course by simply engaging in discussion every week and not turning in any work. Another who implemented pass/no pass grading for multiple skills-based assignments noticed that grades were becoming inflated because *pass* was being converted to *A* in her system. A third who used a system of ✓-, ✓, ✓+ for low-stakes assignments noticed that students' grades were lower than expected and found out that her grading software was converting ✓ into 50%, which ultimately translated into an F for each instance.

The most important thing to establish first is the point system you will use—it's like choosing one currency to commit to. Ultimately, everything in your class will be converted into that currency, so it helps to plan for it at the outset. If you are required to assign letter grades at the end of each semester, figure out what numbers correspond to each letter grade. In the United States, 100-point grading systems are common (100–90 = A, 89–80 = B, 79–70 = C, 69–60 = D, 59–0 = F). Some universities use a 4-point scale (4.0 = A, 3.0 = B, 2.0 = C, 1.0 = D). Whatever your system, stick to it for all of the grades you assign. If you use a 100-point system, make all of your grades multiples of 10 or 100. If you use a 4-point scale, make all of your grades multiples of 4. Instructors sometimes don't even realize that they are setting up different systems in their course when they introduce pass/no pass; ✓-, ✓, ✓+; or other systems into a classroom, and at the end of a grading period, they find themselves with the equivalent of a bill that arrives in a mixture of pesos, yen, and dollars that they have to convert into one currency.

If you consider yourself a stereotypical math-phobic artiste, get help setting up and testing your system. There are a number of excellent automated grading systems available online, or your institution may have one integrated into your learning management system. But even if—or especially if—the system is fully automated, it is wise to invest some time into understanding how that system makes its calculations. Fully understanding how grades are calculated in your system can help you field questions or grievances from students should they arise later in the semester.

Below are a few tips for setting up your grading system:

▶ Ask your department chair or a colleague teaching the same course if there is a numerical grading template you can use that helps with the calculations. Something that has been set up and tested may save you a lot of grief.

▶ Be sure that your calculations reflect the categories that are on your syllabus. If homework is worth 30%, it needs to stay at 30% of the final grade, whether there are ten or twenty homework assignments.

▶ Continue to use ✓-, ✓, ✓+, or an alternate notation you have developed if you feel it is more appropriate for low-stakes assignments. Just be sure that you and your students know what the point values are for each check mark or other notation that you give.

▶ Integrate pass/no pass grading into your system carefully, if you use it. One method that does not artificially inflate or depress grades is to enter only *no pass* grades, without entering *pass* grades. (For example, if Amira does not pass her complementary color schemes quiz, which is fundamental and essential knowledge for the course, she gets a zero, which counts as an F. Mieki passes and does not get a letter grade or any points added to her grade—simply a notation that she passed. Mieki's ultimate grade will be based on the projects— including the contextualized application of her knowledge of complementary color schemes. Amira, however, will have an F factored into her final grade since she has not demonstrated knowledge of these basic skills.) This sets up the baseline expectation that students will master certain skills—that they will not be rewarded for simply mastering vocabulary lists, for being able to save a file in the correct format, or for identifying complementary colors on the color wheel. Their graded work is based on quality, or integration of skills. Using this system, the grade is only affected if the student does not pass (in which case they should be allowed to redo those assignments until they do pass.)

▶   Spot-check your system to make sure that you are placing the right value on specific aspects of performance. For example, if 40% of your grade is homework, but you only enter two grades into that category, each of those assignments is actually going to be worth 20% of the grade, which is likely not what you intended.

▶   Test your system by entering fictional students and numbers into it. Check with your department chair whether these fictional students with specific fictional grading profiles should pass your course, and then adjust your system accordingly. When these types of students come up in real life, you can be confident that you can rely on your grading system. Some examples of what these profiles might look like include:

- The student who was absent one-third of the time and did not turn in half of the homework, but managed to eke out a B on the big final project.

- The student who shows up, follows all directions, and completes all assignments to an acceptable degree, but cannot earn a passing grade on the larger projects.

Tip 12

Ungraded Assignments

When students are given regular ungraded assignments, whether free-writing or an ungraded quiz (the possibilities are endless), there tends to be a measurable overall increase in attendance and performance in the course.[9] Such activities help foster a teaching and learning environment that values and nurtures student learning and development. Activities also transfer the responsibility of learning to the students—and they can even be fun. As Eric Booth puts it in *The Music Teaching Artist's Bible*:

> We may apply a lot of effort to many of the tasks that pass for learning in institutional settings—memorization, skill development, performing a task, regurgitating and applying information—but play is the natural and faster route to mastery of new skills, new information, and greater accomplishment.[10]

While ungraded assignments may not always possess an element of play, they can help to complement and counterbalance other quantitative and summative aspects of the course.

Consider the following ideas for incorporating ungraded work into your course:

► Have students collaborate on problem-based projects in class. Some examples include:

  • Rearranging the lines of a jumbled poem to its original form

  • Sketching the missing half of a famous painting or image

  • Translating one art form into another (e.g., If this painting were a Beckettian monologue, what would it say? What would this sculpture sound like as a saxophone riff?)

  • Incorporating reflective discussion about how and why choices were made

► Promote activities where every person in the class collaborates to write a short story, paint a painting, create a photographic collage, or write and perform a play.

► Invite students to create pieces of art that are intentionally bad or unappealing. Include discussions about aesthetics and taste. Incorporate the language of the discipline.

► Have students spend a timed portion of each class working on their art; encourage nonstop work and stream of consciousness. Students should not be required to share this work although it may lead to a project or body of work that is shared.

FIGURE 10. *THE BOOK OF TENNYSON* BY SAMI TUTONE

Tip 13

Scaffolding Learning Tasks

Students can often feel overwhelmed when learning a new technique or when seeking to fine-tune the skills they already possess. When we scaffold learning tasks, we provide support to students so that they can accomplish a task *that they would otherwise not be able to accomplish on their own.* This scaffolding can be done by providing strong instructional support when students are beginning to learn a new skill, or by breaking learning into small, manageable steps and giving students tools to help them accomplish a task. For example, a scaffolded assignment to create a brochure might include steps on defining the purpose and audience (perhaps with guiding questions on a form that they fill out), selecting appropriate content (with a short list of criteria to help them make the best selections), choosing a layout (perhaps from three choices), and then roughing out and finalizing the brochure. For a second brochure assignment, the steps could be condensed until students are able to work through the process alone without the prior guidance. This gradual removal of the scaffolding from the process may take place over one semester's course, or for more complex processes, it may take place over an entire degree program.

When you carefully scaffold projects for students, your workload may increase, especially at the beginning of the semester. You will be giving frequent, detailed feedback and grades at various early stages to ensure that students are on track. The payoff at the end of the semester should be big, however, as there will likely be fewer student projects that go awry early in the process. You may also find that you need to decrease the number of projects you ask your students to complete as a trade-off with more carefully scaffolded projects.

Toward the end of the semester or project, the instructor should be more of a consultant or colleague, perhaps more frequently asking questions about a student's work than giving guidance or advice, since most of the feedback and guidance has been given at the beginning of the semester or project.

Here are a few things to keep in mind when you scaffold assignments for students:

▶ Consider collaborating on small assignments with students to build their skills. If the learning goal is, for example, to draw a representational human hand, construct an assignment where you participate in the students' early work. This can be done by demonstrating your own process of drawing a hand, but it can also include co-drawing, where you and a student collaborate on a sketch. Connect your own in-class contributions to discussions about discipline-specific concerns such as proportion, shadow, and depth of field. In this example, as the students' work progresses, the instructor's co-drawing should slowly yield to the students drawing entirely on their own.

▶ Modulate the timing and amount of guidance, and do not be overly committed to your initial plans. Evidence shows that too much guidance in the beginning can be counterproductive.[11] Use simple tools—like minute-papers—where students are asked at the end of class if the guidance they are receiving is too much, not enough, or just right. Adjust your guidance accordingly with the goal of ultimately removing this scaffolding by the end of the course.

▸ Let the students know what they can expect at the beginning, middle, and end in terms of your guidance, encouragement, and support. An example of how to communicate this might be: "In the beginning, expect me to _____. In the middle, I will be doing less and more _____. Toward the end, I will _____."

▸ Incorporate metacognitive scaffolding where students are prompted to reflect on their own development as the work progresses. This helps students understand their own process while allowing them to visualize how they will continue to evolve.[12]

Tip 14

Soliciting Feedback

Usually, we think of assessment in terms of instructors grading and giving feedback to the students. But feedback on the course itself and on our own teaching is crucial to the ongoing enterprise of effective teaching and learning. To this end, it can be helpful to think about how you will solicit feedback on your course and on your teaching as you plan your semester.

Most of us are mandated to solicit student evaluations of teaching in our courses at some point in our teaching career. Some of us give them in every course, every semester. These can provide useful information when looking back on the semester, but student evaluations of teaching are often riddled with challenges. First, they often provide unhelpful or irrelevant data. As Philip Stark, professor of statistics at University of California, Berkeley, points out:

> Student teaching evaluations may be influenced by factors that have nothing to do with effectiveness, such as the gender, ethnicity, and attractiveness of the instructor. Students seem to make snap judgments about instructors that have nothing to do with teaching effectiveness, and to rely on those judgments when asked about teaching effectiveness.[13]

Second, they are often not designed by faculty and are not specific to the course being taught. Third, they offer only summative feedback. While summative feedback can guide us in the design of future courses, it doesn't allow us to modify anything to benefit the students who just completed the evaluation. Finally, faculty often rely too heavily on these evaluations when reflecting on their own teaching, or they become disheartened by a few negative comments.

Review your institution's student teaching evaluation forms. If they do not yield the constructive feedback you want, design your own supplemental evaluations and ask students to complete them periodically during the semester. The feedback you receive will be specific to your course, and can help you identify and address problem areas of critical course content before they manifest as poor grades. Furthermore, students will be more invested in the course—and in their own learning—if their input into the process is valued.

When soliciting feedback on your teaching and course, bear in mind the following:

▸ Keep it short. Students should be able to complete surveys or other instruments in five minutes or less.

▸ Keep the questions simple, such as:

- What is one thing about this course that's going well?
- What is one thing about this course that isn't going well?
- What is one thing about this course that I can improve?

▸ Consider multiple choice questions that allow students to expand on their answer. For example:

• Which of the following learning activities have been most/least helpful to your understanding of the material so far? Rank your answers and add comments in the text box below.

· Textbook readings

· Lectures

· Case study discussions

· Presentations

▸ Make sure you share the results with students, or at least what you will change as a result of their feedback. This helps students be invested in the process and in the course.

▸ Consider using a web-based tool. Google forms, for example, will allow you to easily capture and share the data from your evaluations visually.

▸ Make it clear on your syllabus that you will seek feedback from students throughout the semester.

Part I Supplementary Resources

Further reading on course design

Alber, Rebecca. "6 Scaffolding Strategies to Use With Your Students."
　　Edutopia. May 24, 2011. https://www.edutopia.org/blog/
　　scaffolding-lessons-six-strategies-rebecca-alber.
Strategies for scaffolding in higher education classrooms can be found in
this article and can be easily adapted to postsecondary contexts, even
though *Edutopia* targets K–12 teachers.

Angelo, Thomas A., and K. Patricia Cross. *Classroom Assessment
　　Techniques: A Handbook for College Teachers*. San Francisco: Jossey-
　　Bass, 1993.
This is the original bible for "CATS," or classroom assessment techniques,
which are practical, easy-to-implement activities that help instructors find
out how well students are learning.

Booth, Eric. "Creating the Playground." Chap. 10 in *The Music Teaching
　　Artist's Bible: Becoming a Virtuoso Educator*. Oxford: Oxford
　　University Press, 2009.
Chapter 10 is an inspiring reference for bringing the power of play into
your course, whether music or other disciplines. The entire book is a rich
resource for creative approaches to instruction that can be easily translated to any field.

Fink, L. Dee. *Creating Significant Learning Experiences: An Integrated Approach to Designing College Courses*. San Francisco: Jossey-Bass, 2013.

This book provides a comprehensive, practical approach to course design. An abbreviated version of the approach, also by L. Dee Fink, is also available online as "Idea Paper #42" at *IDEA* (https://www.ideaedu.org).

Lewis, Karron G. "Using Midsemester Student Feedback and Responding to It." *New Directions for Teaching and Learning* 2001, no. 87 (2001): 33. https://doi.org/10.1002/tl.26.

This article includes helpful examples of feedback questions.

Nilson, Linda. *Specifications Grading: Restoring Rigor, Motivating Students, and Saving Faculty Time*. Sterling, VA: Stylus Publishing, 2015.

This smart book offers an innovative approach to grading based primarily on pass/no pass grading, which fosters student intrinsic motivation. Instructors who are confident that their courses are integrated, and that the work they require of students is a good measure of learning, may find this approach worthwhile.

Rand, Glenn, and Richard Zakia. *Teaching Photography: Tools for the Imaging Educator*. Burlington, MA: Focal Press, 2006.

Although written specifically for photography instructors in higher education, many of this book's insights on matters from pre- to post-semester are easily adaptable to any creative discipline.

Wiggins, Grant P., and Jay McTighe. *Understanding by Design.*
    Alexandria, VA: Association for Supervision and Curriculum
    Development, 2008.
This workbook provides an accessible model for backward course design
with detailed activities and suggestions to help with big picture planning as
well as focused assignment design.

FIGURE 11. *UNTITLED* BY ROBIN ESCHNER

PART II

During the Semester

Part two is for grab and go ideas in the middle of the semester.

Communicating Goals

So much of the success of our assessment and teaching relies on the expectations we set up with our students. If they understand the hows and whys of assessment, they can be partners in the process.

15. Making Grading Expectations Clear
16. A Mutual Understanding of Progress
17. Clarifying Teaching Methods
18. Choice of Graded Projects
19. Office Hours

Emphasizing Process over Results

Being an artist is not about creating excellent work 100% of the time; it is about establishing an excellent process for creating work. By understanding the steps of the creative process and what successful passage through them looks like in the classroom, faculty can better isolate skills and practices to be graded and encouraged.

20. Making Creative Process Explicit
21. Redefining Effort
22. Problem Finding
23. Generating Ideas and Brainstorming
24. Aha! Moments
25. Grading and Mistakes

Teaching Content and Skills

Discrete skills and disciplinary knowledge are essential tools for all artists.

Rubrics

These teaching and learning tools, when carefully written, will guide the learning process by defining goals.

The Critique

The core of assessment in most artistic disciplines, the critique should be carefully planned and tailored for each context.

Tip 15

Making Grading Expectations Clear

Establishing clear grading criteria and practices can be challenging in the arts, partly due to the ephemeral nature of the oral critique, which is so central to teaching art. (See tip 3.) In the long history of oral critiques, faculty in the arts have rarely been taught to *clarify* standards to students at the outset; they seem to expect the standards to emerge organically in the discussions that arise. This is not to say that faculty in the arts don't have grading criteria; they just tend not to make them known as explicitly as in some other disciplines.

For example, we rarely provide real, *achievable* examples of completed, graded projects. We mostly look at the best work of past or established artists, not examples from former students. And if neither achievable examples nor rubrics are provided, it makes completing assignments more difficult for students, and ultimately, grading more difficult for faculty.

Clarify your grading expectations at the beginning—of the course, and of each assignment—so that students can understand them and you can more easily hold them to those expectations. Consider what you value

FIGURE 12. *THE ROYAL COURTS OF JUSTICE* BY SAMI TUTONE

most and emphasize those points at the beginning of the semester. For example, if participation (see tip 29) is something you value (and thus grade), clarify expectations for student engagement at the onset of the semester. And let students know what they can expect of you. Such statements do not have to be overly detailed or specific, but should simply outline general expectations. Communicate your expectations early and often—more globally in the syllabus and in a more detailed way as you introduce each assignment.

- Adjust your grading expectations to focus on the essentials of a given assignment.

- Decide on the few expectations that are the most important and distill those to bullet points for passing and not passing work.

- Use realistic, achievable examples of work to clarify your expectations.

- Check in with students as they progress through each assignment, revisiting your grading expectations and making sure they are addressing them.

- Let students know, emphatically and individually, that you have high standards and that you also have faith that they can meet those standards, even if it takes a couple of tries. This message may be especially important for students who feel that they are not part of the dominant culture of academia—and who are more likely to drop out of a program of study than dominant culture students. For more on the phenomenon of stereotype vulnerability, see Claude Steele's book in the further reading section.

▶ Use rubrics!

▶ Use checklists, especially for longer, multi-stage assignments. If you are teaching online, you might also use your learning management system's tools to help students keep track of important steps in any assignment.

▶ Clarify your expectations for student engagement with a statement in your syllabus like the following sample: *You will experience success in this course if you remain engaged in weekly discussions, complete technical exercises and major photography projects on time, and approach critique sessions with genuine interest in helping yourself and your peers improve.*

▶ Clarify what students should expect from the instructor with a statement in your syllabus like the following sample: *To help you experience success in this course, I will always provide assistance in your understanding of technical and theoretical concepts. I will also work with you individually as you develop the skills necessary for successful completion of this course. Finally, I will strive to provide a safe and intellectually stimulating learning environment.*

Tip 16

A Mutual Understanding of Progress

Too often, grades are given as final declarations of success or failure. They are summative (closed comments on what has already been done) instead of formative (helping to inform current or future work on the path to a broader goal). These declarations tend to be unidirectional. They neither invite students into a discussion about their understanding of the assessment, nor do they provide the opportunity to continue working on those concepts and skills that are being assessed. This grade-and-move-on approach is detrimental to development, especially in courses where the skills and concepts build on each other. Without solid foundations, skills and concepts learned later will likely be weakened, leading to further struggle. Furthermore, this summative grading practice only serves to reinforce students' ideas of their limited or constrained role in the learning process.

To break away from summative, unidirectional grading, consider using grades as openings for students to discuss how they are meeting (or not meeting) grading expectations. If they are meeting expectations, great! Use grades as an opportunity to recognize their successes. If they aren't meeting expectations, use grades to alert them to this *and* to allow them to make adjustments or corrections. Allow them to revisit, revise, and relearn, either before or after they move on to new content. This latter approach is in line with mastery learning[14] as it emphasizes learning until a skill has been mastered, instead of learning until all of the assignments have been, for better or worse, completed and graded. Using grades in this formative way will reduce student fear of grades, increase their investment and ownership of the grading process, and ultimately improve student performance in your classes.

▸ Frame your grades as questions to the students, asking whether they believe they met the expectations of the course.

▸ After giving summative grades, build opportunities for students to demonstrate (in a short essay, during office hours, etc.) their understanding of their grades' meanings and describe how they can correct for errors in future work.

▸ At several points throughout the semester, ask students to reflect on the grades they were given. Have them state how they have learned from their grades and how they have since improved or mastered those previously assessed skills or concepts.

▸ When students have not earned a passing grade on an assignment or project, deliver that grade as *not yet*, instead of D or F, and ask them to resubmit until they do meet the expectations.

Tip 17

Clarifying Teaching Methods

One of the most common instruction-related requests by students is for clearer, more explicit organization of the course.[15] Having a clear syllabus and sticking to its timeline is not quite enough. Nor is it enough to review the syllabus on the first day and ask if there are any questions. Ideally, students know from the beginning how the course will be taught and how their work and performance will be graded. Will it be mostly lecture? Will there be regular small-group activities? Will there be problem-based learning, role playing, or peer instruction? How will these different approaches be used and why? And how specifically will students' performance be assessed and graded? Will formative feedback—in the form of written comments—always accompany grades? How might the mechanism of grading differ from activity to activity? The answers to these questions will play an important role in shaping the climate of the course and have a direct impact on student learning.[16] This climate begins to take shape on the first day.

Here are some suggestions for clarifying your teaching methods to students:

▸ Model the various teaching methods and use them as ice breakers on the first day. For example, if your course is a mixture of lecture with

FIGURE 13. *SPRINGEESE I* BY MARY SWANN

frequent student interaction, and some studio time where you check in with students one-on-one, make time to give students a taste of each of those activities on the first day.

▶ Use a fishbowl activity to model various teaching methods. Join a small group of students in an inner circle with everyone else surrounding you in the structure of an outer circle. You and the students in the inner circle engage in abbreviated versions of various teaching and learning activities, such as lecture, peer critique, student-led discussion, or think-pair-share. The students in the outer circle observe and take notes on the demonstration, then share questions or concerns that can be discussed to clarify the virtues of certain methods.

▶ Students should have a chance to ask questions and participate in the discussion about the proposed teaching methods. Ask for and encourage feedback. Let students know you'll be requesting and welcoming their input throughout the semester.

▶ Be flexible. Students often have great suggestions about how to teach something differently while achieving the same instructional goal.

▶ Discuss some of the reasons why certain approaches will be used and what learning goals you hope to achieve as a result.

▶ Discuss what types of active learning, if any, will be graded or counted toward a grade. Share rubrics or other grading criteria.

Tip 18

Choice of Graded Projects

Is my class boring?

A perennial challenge for any instructor is to design and teach an engaging course. One way to do this is to offer students a choice of graded assignments. Providing choices helps prevent a course from becoming rote or predictable (for students and instructors) and gives students a chance to co-create their learning experience. Students can also feel a greater sense of personal investment and responsibility for the grade when they have chosen their own project. Students who are given choices tend to show an increase in motivation and performance, and they tend to more readily accept challenging tasks.[17]

But it can sometimes seem like there aren't that many options for students in the arts when it comes to making choices about projects. While students' individual work is the result of countless aesthetic choices, their assignments can often feel monolithic: work on your short stories, complete your sketches, revise your librettos. While these kinds of directives are often necessary, it can be helpful for students to have more nuanced options. Offering students choices about topics or skill focus, for example, can invite them to look deeper, tap into their intrinsic motivation, take more control over their learning, and push their limits. It can also allow them to pull back and polish something that needs extra attention. When students help shape their own pathway through the semester, it makes the course more engaging. Students can progress more as a result.

▶ Offer choices of small assignments that allow students to focus on narrowly defined areas in which they're interested, or that they are having trouble understanding. In a sculpture class, for example, students can be given the choice to complete a relatively brief project that focuses on only one of the following: balance, proportion, theme, movement, repetition, relief, or negative space. Students can be required to articulate, in a paper or in a class presentation and discussion, how their work, or their peers' work, explores a specific aspect.

▶ Choices should be finite rather than open-ended. Give students just a few options, perhaps no more than six, to choose from. Giving an overwhelming number of choices tends to be counterproductive.[18]

▶ Have students select specific components of an assignment in order to blend negotiable and nonnegotiable elements. For example, in photography, students could choose whether to select shutter speed, aperture, or focal length from a longer list of negotiable technical aspects as their emphasis. The instructor then emphasizes the student-selected component when grading. This way, the instructor can ensure that core objectives and content are always included.

▶ Make sure that the options presented to students are as equitable and balanced as possible in terms of the estimated amount of work or engagement required.

▶ Provide students a timeline for switching projects if the one they choose fails to hold their interest or proves not to be that challenging.

▶ If the semester is already underway, look for opportunities for choices that may already exist.

▶ If you're concerned about departmental mandates for instruction, check in with the chair or program director. You may have more leeway than you think.

Tip 19

Office Hours

Most of us are required to hold office hours. In addition, we often make ourselves available to students more often and in more settings than the regularly scheduled places and times. Office hours provide an opportunity for students to develop their understanding in a way that is not always possible in the classroom or on their own. It often seems to be the case, however, that those students who need the most help rarely or never show up or take advantage of our time outside of the classroom.

Student engagement with the larger spectrum of the artistic process is the root issue here, and it is a critical aspect of the assessment process in any creative discipline. This engagement includes work done on projects beyond the confines of classroom time, including during office hours. Consider your own spectrum of engagement, and within that, how much time you dedicate to connecting with peers or mentors. For example, a writer may spend an hour every morning putting pen to paper and meet with a group of peers for feedback every week.

Think about students you had in your courses last semester or within the past year. Compare the students who struggled, but in the end fared well, to those who struggled and did not fare well. Consider which students applied themselves outside of class hours, either by taking

FIGURE 14. *INSOMNIANAS* BY GARY HAWKINS, WARREN WILSON COLLEGE, NC

advantage of your office hours or open labs where a teaching assistant was present. That additional discussion, coaching, or instructional time often makes all the difference.

So how do we get students—especially those who are struggling—to take advantage of our office hours? Here are a few tips to get you started:

▸ Don't simply advertise your office hours on the first day of class and in your syllabi. Make the purpose of office hours clear and ask students to bring specific questions (some students may not know what office hours are). Consider creating special topics or themes for office hours, for example, "research for Project 2." Regularly remind students about your availability.

▸ When grading higher-stakes projects, consider the time the students spend working in labs or studios outside of class. Assuming you are using rubrics, add a line that specifies an individual conference (or multiple conferences) with you, either during open labs or during your regularly scheduled office hours. This is their chance to demonstrate to you that they are not only working on their projects outside of class time, but also taking the process of project development seriously. It is your chance to provide them guidance *and* to model the kinds of feedback exchanges they will need to continue in their lives as professional artists.

▸ Try holding office hours with dyads and triads of students for collaborative work, instead of just one-on-one.

▸ Consider requiring all students to attend an office hour at some point during the first few weeks of the semester, perhaps connected to one of their first projects. This requirement is especially helpful in the case of struggling students. A meeting breaks the ice and makes it easier for them to come back.

▸ If possible, bend your schedule to meet with those students who need the most help, especially at the beginning of the semester.

Tip 20

Making Creative Process Explicit

So . . . what are we doing again? Am I supposed to choose one of the ideas I just presented? Or do I have to come up with a new one? Can't you just tell me which one is best?

An instructor who has spent an hour facilitating a critique would understandably be discouraged by a student response like the one above. To the instructor, it could not be more obvious that he has critiqued students' initial ideas in order to help them refine their thinking and progress to the next stage of a project—he has been helping them through a critical phase of the creative process. Why would he otherwise critique them? But that student may simply be impatient to complete the project at hand. The intention behind the critique may be lost on this student because the instructor has not explicitly communicated its purpose and value.

Many instructors have internalized their own creative process so much that they are not even aware of its steps. But it is important to deconstruct and articulate these internalized steps through various teaching and learning activities, including critique, in order to teach and assess them. When you define what success looks like at various discrete points of the process, you can give students more focused feedback along the way. And most important of all, students can track their own progress and make better sense of your feedback at various stages.

Creativity guru R. Keith Sawyer developed an integrated model of the creative process, based on extensive study and observations. According to his model, most creative people go through steps that roughly correspond to problem finding, acquiring knowledge, gathering related knowledge, incubation, generating ideas, combining ideas, selecting ideas, and externalizing ideas.[19] You probably have your own names for the steps of your process. There may be fewer or more than eight. And whatever process you use, it is likely not a lockstep linear checklist of things to do but more a description of landmarks—some of which may be revisited—on a general road map through the creative process.

Here are some tips for explicitly teaching creative process:

▸   Name and define each step as clearly as possible. When we name concepts, it is easier to talk about and assess them.

▸   Answer the question: How do you assign value to each step of the process? Once you have established the goals of each step, you have a benchmark against which to assess students' progress. For example, if the goal for the generating ideas step is quantity and variety, your assessment should be based on how much work the student produces and how varied that work is.

▶ Link classroom activities often to the creative-process steps that you have defined. Ask students "Where are we now in the creative process?"

▶ Model your own creative process in class. Verbalize your thought process and link your thoughts to various creative-process steps as you demonstrate how you approach a creative challenge.

▶ Every three weeks or so, have students do a ten-minute reflection on their creative process. Follow up by having them trade papers and respond to each other or engage them in a large-group discussion. Possible questions:

   • Which steps are most difficult for you? Which are easiest? Why?

   • What are some strategies you have discovered to push through the difficult stages?

   • What are some ways to brainstorm ideas?

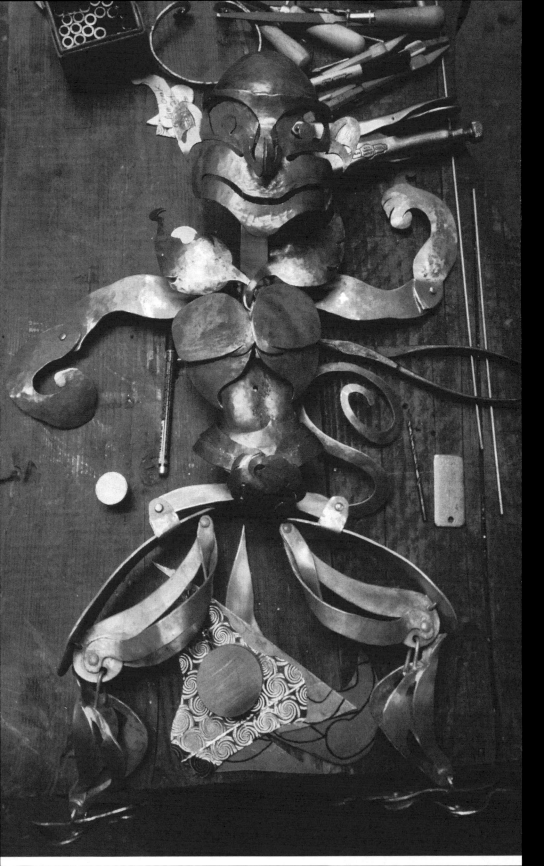

Tip 21

Redefining Effort

"A for effort!" We know the meaning behind the line: the result was unsuccessful.

Grading for effort seems to be particularly prevalent in creative fields, probably because as creative practitioners, we know that while hard work is crucial to success and will pay off eventually, the result of any single burst of effort may not look successful. We crave a way to communicate to our students *you are going about your work in the right way, even though the result this time was not what you hoped for.*

As we have said before in this book, the key to assessment is making what you value visible. But effort, though highly valued, is particularly difficult to make visible. Instructors often claim they can see effort in the visual work that students do, but what we see can be misleading. Unrefined-looking pieces may have actually required tremendous time and effort from the student; labored-looking pieces may be the result of a lot of effort, but perhaps the wrong kind of effort. Conversely, beautiful work

FIGURE 15 (OPPOSITE). *MONKEY FIGURE* (FROM *INNER CITY TOTEM*) BY BETH SOUSA, ACADEMY OF ART UNIVERSITY, CA may come from students with extensive previous experience who expended hardly any effort at all.

To encourage all students, regardless of natural talent, to work hard *and* smart, we recommend grading on *process* rather than effort. While effort refers to the sheer force that is being exerted, process implies that there is some path or organization to govern the effort. Comments on process carry less inherent judgment. "You did not complete the process" will likely invite fewer defensive reactions than "you did not put enough effort into it." Below are some ways to make effort more observable as part of a process:

▶   Have students include process books or journals with their projects. These can include early ideas, notes from critique, or even photos of them working through different phases of the project. This book could be completed in any medium, electronic or print. You can assess documentation of each stage of the process as well as students' reflection on the process. This assessment can be incorporated into the project grade or into a participation and discussion grade.

▶   Break projects into stages and communicate concrete expectations about what students need to show each week as evidence of their progress. This may be a journal entry, ten photographs, forty thumbnails, before and after revision of a piece, a response to peer review, or any number of other pieces of evidence. Advanced students might define the stages and set their own goals.

▸ Create some pass/no pass assignments where students are merely expected to put a certain amount of time into a project. If you do these in class, you can observe the time that students need to put in. If the assignment is outside of class, you could have them document their progress every half hour with a time-stamped photograph.

▸ Empathize with students who say they have put an exceptional amount of effort into a project or assignment, but make it clear from the beginning of the semester that you will be assessing their process.

Tip 22

Problem Finding

Now that you understand the assignment, let's get started.

So begin most assignments: the instructor defines the parameters as clearly as he can, and the students *do the work*. Well-defined assignments support good learning. And in courses where you are focusing on the development of a particular skill, a strong assignment probably includes a very clear, solvable problem so that the students know exactly what to focus on. But to foster creative development, we need to be careful not to do too much of the work for students. To prepare them to work in the real world, and indeed, to increase their chances of becoming professional artists, we need to give students opportunities to engage in the earliest and often neglected part of the creative process: problem *finding*.

Working artists seldom have externally defined *assignments* to respond to. They usually need to spend plenty of time defining—or finding—the problem themselves before even beginning what we often think of as the *work* of a project. A commission to paint the Manhattan skyline in a fresh way, for example, does not present itself with clear guidelines and criteria; that one last short story for the soon-to-be-published book doesn't come with an outline; a creative brief contains plenty of information, but does not tell an art director what to do in response to it.

Even the thesis requirement in graduate school does not come as a detailed assignment to complete.

A notable study on how artists produce creative work concluded that painters who spent more time defining a visual problem—in this case, arranging and rearranging the elements of a still life—produced more creative work than those who did the inverse and spent more of their time just painting. Interestingly, a follow-up study with these same artists found that the painters who had taken more time with problem finding were much more likely to be working artists several years after graduation. Subsequent studies on writers and math students yielded similar results: people who spend time defining a problem do more high-quality and creative work than those who begin their project with an ill-defined problem.[20] Cultivating problem-finding skills in our students doesn't mean that we toss all structured assignments out and let students find their own way. It does mean that we should incorporate problem finding into our classes. Here are some examples of how to do that:

▸   Make *find the problem* step one in your assignments. Develop criteria to assess when a problem is found and sufficiently defined. Guide students through the problem-finding process and use these criteria to help them know when they have a well-defined problem to solve. For example, if your assignment is to build a simple website in your basic web design course, the student who says she will "build a website for a band" has a less clearly defined problem than the student who says she will "build an easy-to-update website for a band to include their performance dates, merchandise order links, samples of music, and basic band bio information."

▶ Allow for additional time in the early stage of a project for students to arrange and rearrange its components, before requiring them to jump in to *solve* the problem. Give feedback on, or even grade, the amount of time they spend on this part of the process, or the number of iterations they have gone through to arrive at a solvable problem.

▶ Consider having students work on problem finding individually for a week, then come together as a class to define a consensus problem. You can assess the individual or the group work at this stage of the project. Coming to this consensus ensures that even students who do not have strong problem-finding skills will be able to start the project on equal footing.

▶ Be aware of students who feel like they are spinning their wheels or who may be late with their work, but seem to have been working hard. They may be doing exactly what the successful artists described in the aforementioned study were doing, rearranging the components of the problem. Instructors can help these students understand the importance of problem finding and help them develop strategies to move on to the next phase of a project when it is time. Measuring this problem-finding ability, setting deadlines for it, and explicitly assessing or grading it in the early stages can serve as an early warning system.

Tip 23

Generating Ideas and Brainstorming

The group brainstorming session, which grew out of the advertising world in the 1950s, is an iconic image of creativity for many people. ("Any idea is a good idea! Never criticize an idea in a brainstorm!") Although fine artists and others who consider creativity a more solitary process may scoff at it, the group brainstorm has become a familiar classroom activity in many disciplines, from K–12 to higher ed. Brainstorming is often perceived as an energizing, collaborative diversion—a fun break from the rigor of the usual academic classroom routine. And it seems to have become synonymous with the idea-generation step of the creative process.

But as many instructors who have tried it know, the group brainstorm does not always result in great ideas or in students feeling more confident in their abilities to generate ideas. A brainstorm usually results in massive quantities of unrelated ideas of varied quality (this is pretty much the point), and it can be hard to know how to move forward without breaking that cardinal rule of "every idea is a good idea." Furthermore, shy students, or those who do not think on their feet quickly, can feel inferior in these large brainstorming sessions. An

FIGURE 16. *ALLEGORY (THE BANQUET OF CLEOPATRA)* (FROM ALLEGORY ON LOCATION ASSIGNMENT) BY GLORIA OLIVER, ROCHESTER COMMUNITY AND TECHNICAL COLLEGE, MN

instructor who is trying to assess students' performance in a brainstorming session (like the one described above) may resort to assessing social skills or extroversion more than actual idea generation.

If we remember that the classic brainstorm is only one tool to generate ideas—it is not the step itself—we can actually craft learning activities for this phase of the creative process to more efficiently generate ideas and to include more students. Recent research provides us with good guidance on how to manage the idea-generation phase of a project. It turns out that peer input and feedback can help in the idea-generation phase of a project, but not in the format of a classic "brainstorm." A list of ideas compiled from five solo brainstorms will actually be more creative than a list of the same length generated by the same five people in a group setting.[21] And hearing group dissent and critique of those lists can lead participants to generate even *more* creative ideas. So the group work should occur after the initial solo brainstorming, and it *should* include some critique and discussion of the ideas.

Use the ideas below to help your students become comfortable in the idea-generation phase of the creative process, and to help you focus on what to assess.

▸ Give students questions to spur ideas in the idea-generation phase of a project: How would you solve this if money were no object? How would a seven-year-old solve it? Turn it upside down. Draw five bad ideas, then draw their opposites.

▸ Insist on a certain number of ideas for the idea-generation phase of a project. Hold individual students accountable for the sheer volume, but *also* have them star the three ideas that they think are best.

▶ Use a group session to build on individually generated ideas. Participants can use the "yes and" approach to add to their peers' ideas. Again, assessment can be based on the sheer number or variety of ideas a peer contributes.

▶ Have students discuss and critique their three best ideas with peers, then generate more ideas on their own. Assess this second iteration of ideas for quality as well as quantity.

Tip 24

_____

Aha! Moments

Most artists have experienced the delight that comes from an *aha! moment* when a solution suddenly becomes crystal clear and everything fits together perfectly. These moments often occur in bed, in the bath, or on the bus—when the artist is not consciously focusing on the problem at hand. They seldom occur in a classroom.

This can be frustrating for both instructors and students. Instructors want their students to experience the joy of those moments of insight. They also want to see the exciting ideas that often emerge from them. Students, too, want the joy of those moments. But deadlines and intense focus on the projects at hand often block any possibility for them to occur in the classroom. Both instructors and students unnecessarily relegate the aha! moment to something that occurs outside of school, unrelated to the business of studying art.

If you have read a few of the other tips in this book, you will recognize our recurring mantra: figure out what you value and make it visible to your students. With aha! moments, this may not be possible as they seem so elusive. But current research does provide us with some hints about processes that support and make aha! moments visible.

Aha! moments used to be held up as evidence of the mysterious nature of creativity, evidence that creative ideas come out of the blue. The Romantics of the eighteenth century believed, as R. Keith Sawyer describes it, that "creativity bubbles up from an irrational unconscious and that rational deliberation interferes with the creative process."[22] The unconscious mind certainly plays some role in the creative process, but scientific investigation proves what many creative thinkers have already figured out on their own, that the aha! moment generally follows a predictable sequence of problem-solving steps: defining the problem, wrestling with it, researching it, working very hard to solve it, and finally, taking a break from (or even giving up on) it. This final step of backing away after a lot of hard work seems to create an incubation period that allows the breakthrough to emerge.

Research also suggests that having several problems in this incubation stage at the same time can help.[23] This process holds true for very large problems that one works on for months—or even years—at a time as well as smaller problems, such as puzzles.

Procrastination is the enemy of aha! moments. Students who complete the bulk of the work on their assignments at the last minute sabotage the possibility for aha! moments to emerge before deadlines. By manipulating the timing of the grading and feedback, instructors can coax students into earlier completion of the hard work that is necessary for aha! moments to occur.

▶   Give early grades and feedback on larger projects, and allow students to deepen and improve work before giving a final grade. This allows time and motivation needed for aha! moments to emerge later.

▶ Encourage students to begin work on projects with short bursts of nonstop work to help overcome resistance and procrastination.

▶ Break larger projects into short, intense periods of work.

▶ Revisit work that has already received a final critique. Ask students whether any other insights or aha! moments have emerged since that final critique.

▶ When students are working on a very hard problem in class, have them take a break to work on a second, unrelated problem for ten minutes. Afterward, have students self assess the process. Ask whether they see their own work differently after being pulled into the world of another problem.

Tip 25

Grading and Mistakes

If you don't make mistakes, you aren't really trying.

The quote above is widely attributed to jazz saxophonist Coleman Hawkins, but could have been uttered by almost any artist, anywhere, at any time. Artists must learn to take risks and embrace mistakes. This is one of the few truths that artists can agree on. But in a classroom, it can generate a paradox as grading systems can seem inherently set up to *punish* risk and failure. This is not an easy paradox to reconcile. Research into the importance of risks and mistakes, however, can give us a toehold on establishing a grading system that encourages mistakes and risk-taking.

A description from *Art and Fear* of contrasting final projects in a pair of ceramics classes illustrates how focusing students on quality in final product may actually be detrimental to the processes that yield quality. One group of ceramics students was told to make the *best single piece* they could and present it at the end of the semester. The second group was told to make *as many pieces as they could* over the course of the semester. The most creative work came out of the second group.[24]

No art program wants to graduate students who have portfolios full of mistakes. Students need to edit and refine their work before they show it. But the portfolio work will be stronger if students have made a lot of mistakes along the way. If instructors are constantly grading students on the quality of their final pieces, there is little incentive for a grade-conscious student (or one whose scholarship relies on a strong GPA) to take any risks.

There is an entire course at Pennsylvania State University on taking risks and making mistakes called Failure 101. It is taught by Professor Jack V. Matson who explains the course by saying, "the frequency and intensity of failures is an implicit principle of the course. Getting into a creative mind-set involves a lot of trial and error."[25] Few of us probably have the opportunity to create such a course, but we can glean some ideas from his approach.

Consider the following ways, including some from Failure 101, to incorporate an assessment of students' abilities to take risks and embrace mistakes:

▸ For a final or other high-stakes project, instead of one piece, have students create and finish several. Allow them to choose the one that will be graded on quality, but have a portion of the final grade reflect the mere completion of the other pieces.

▸ Issue each student a "spectacular fail" ticket that they can use to waive a grade on one assignment for which they take a creative risk and are ultimately unsuccessful by the standard assignment

s rain pulls worms for

let the smoke maul the sun
it's clear now what limb
needs to sing ~~the night~~ *e*
which hair needs pummeling
what eye needs feeding ⎰ *see p*
to scout the ground for ⎱
shadows of eel ~~of eye~~ *e*
a (missing luck)
a sharp moon
summon~~ed by the child~~
who walks ~~in old~~ footprints
knees adust with tinder

parameters and criteria. (The spectacular fail ticket should never be used in lieu of work that is missing or simply weak.)

▶   Create a graded assignment like Professor Matson's favorite in his Failure 101 course: construct a résumé based on things that didn't work out and find the meaning and influences these failures have had on your choices.

▶   Dedicate a class meeting to sharing stories of failure, and create a Dia de los Muertos–style altar where students can place remnants of failed projects. This idea was implemented at X (the moonshot company at Alphabet, Google's parent company) when a manager perceived that many employees "were carrying heavy emotional baggage"[26] due to defunct or failed projects.

▶   In the early stage of a project, insist on a number of ideas, including a certain number of bad ideas. Issue a grade based on the sheer number of ideas and inclusion of bad ones.

Tip 26

Contemplative Practice

Sometimes, in spite of our most sincere efforts to teach well, to incorporate transparent grading practices, and to involve students in their own learning, students have trouble focusing and sustaining effort. The challenge here may not lie in our teaching practices or grading systems, but with students who may be too stressed and distracted to benefit as much as they could from feedback and grades.

The employment of brief contemplative practices, such as meditation or a simple breathing exercise, can indeed help students focus, and get them in a space where they are ready to learn—a space where all of the careful preparation you have done for teaching has a chance to be effective. Research shows that these practices improve students' ability to maintain preparedness and orient attention, process information quickly and accurately, and support the development of creativity.[27] Such practices can thus create a climate that helps students generate new ideas and engage more effectively with course work—as well as with critiques, grades, and other feedback.

The practice of art is itself a contemplative practice, but distracted or stressed students may not experience it as such. As the novelist Salman

Rushdie put it, the creative act "is made at the boundary between self and the world, and during this creative act this borderline softens, turns penetrable and allows the world to flow into the artist and the artist into the world."[28] Students who are perpetually distracted or focused on just passing the course are probably less likely to be able to experience this kind of engagement.

Try the following techniques before in-class activities. Have the transition between these activities and class work be as seamless as possible, with little or no conversation or reflection. It may take several attempts before students notice any quieting of the mind or an increased ability to focus more deeply.

- Embodied Walking (ten to fifteen minutes): Walk slowly, single file, in a large loop or circle (outside, ideally), and focus on the physical sensations of the body's movement—the shift of weight from heel to toe, inhaling and exhaling, the gentle swaying of the body. Eyes should be open, gaze lowered slightly. Notice whenever the mind wanders away and then gently return awareness to walking.

- Focused Meditation (five to fifteen minutes): Find a comfortable sitting posture with straightened spine, eyes slightly open and silently count exhalations from one to ten. Breathe naturally. Try to focus completely on counting each exhalation with each number lasting the length of the breath. Whenever the mind wanders, return awareness to counting the exhalations, beginning again with the number one. If you are uncomfortable leading an exercise like this, you can find many recordings online to guide your students (and yourself) through a short focusing exercise.

▸ Journaling (five to fifteen minutes): (a) Write without any goal, purpose, or subject. The only rule is to not stop writing. (b) Write nonstop about an object (a brick) or an idea (beauty) and attempt to exhaust all associations.

Tip 27

Famous Artists' Early Work

When we encounter a powerful work of art, or a body of work by a famous artist, it's easy to forget the countless hours, rough drafts, and false starts that eventually led to the work before us. *How did she do it?* we may wonder, indulging an assumption or belief that the artist has always created such transcendent work. It's especially easy for students to forget that every artist was once a beginner, struggling to learn the basics of the form. Students who engage in this line of thought can become impatient and want to skip important, developmental stages. By introducing students to examples of early work by well-known artists, we can help them see firsthand the undeniable evidence of process and development—and why it's so important. The famous artist becomes a little more human and approachable. The path of the artist can thus seem more within reach.

Students can also acquire a longer view of their own development. They can better appreciate that the work they're doing right now, in your class, is likely their own early work. Within this broader context, grades can be seen more as cairns marking a mountain path and less as proclamations of talent or potential.

FIGURE 18. *OPHELIA IN THE RIVER* (FROM ALLEGORY ON LOCATION ASSIGNMENT) BY
SAMANTHA COHRAN, ROCHESTER COMMUNITY AND TECHNICAL COLLEGE, MN

Below are a few ways to incorporate early work by successful artists to demonstrate the importance of process:

▸   Juxtapose an artist's early work with later work and ask students to identify which elements become more emphasized as the artist's skills progress. Which elements become less emphasized? What new elements, styles, or approaches appear?

▸   Explore examples outside of your discipline. Using the questions in the tip above, students can explore, for example, the 1967 short film *The Big Shave*, created by Martin Scorsese when he was a graduate student at New York University, or the very early paintings of Pablo Picasso (*Le Picador*, 1890) and Salvador Dalí (*Landscape Near Figueras*, 1910). The book *Songs in the Rough* by Stephen Bishop provides early rough drafts of famous lyrics to some of rock and roll's most well-known songs. Museums can also provide examples and artifacts of the early work of artists of all stripes.

▸   Ask students to identify three unsolved questions in light of the following quotation from Rainer Maria Rilke's *Letters to a Young Poet*:

> Have patience with everything that remains unsolved in your heart. Try to love the questions themselves, like locked rooms and like books written in a foreign language. Do not now look for the answers. They cannot now be given to you because you could not live them. It is a question of experiencing everything. At present you need to live the question.[29]

▸ Encourage students to save their own early drafts for future reference. This can help remind students of the effort that went into their work and the drafts provide a fossil record of upward trajectory and development.[30]

▸ Have students imagine that they are wildly successful artists twenty years from now. Have them write a letter of advice from their future successful self to their current self. What wisdom would they have to share? What regrets might they have? What lessons have they learned? How has their art evolved?

Tip 28

_____

The Artist-Apprentice Dynamic

The stereotype of the artist as anti-establishment and somehow existing outside of institutionalized structure can sometimes complicate grading and assessment. The student can become convinced that any assessment is merely a function of a rigid academy that the real artist is supposed to reject. Such a student can exhibit skepticism—and even hostility—toward any and all feedback.

Even the most constructive and well-intentioned feedback can be seen as a personal affront and can serve as further evidence of some kind of institutionalized attempt to thwart, diminish, or limit creativity. One way to normalize assessment is to have students explore the history of apprenticeship in your specific discipline—or in the arts in general. It can be revelatory for students to understand that almost all successful and famous artists worked persistently for many years, almost always studying for a period of time with a more experienced artist, before achieving a level of mastery. With such an understanding in mind, the student may be more capable of seeing assessment as simply part of the path, and thus a way to learn and grow.

Here are a few ways to approach this exploration:

▸ Personalize the path of the artist. Tell stories about your own kinds of apprenticeship, who your teachers were, your experiences as a student, and how you learned: from assessment, feedback in any form, experiences, research, travel, and so on. Emphasize how feedback, critique, and dialogue are part of a bigger apprenticeship picture. Here is one example of an apprenticeship, which the poet and translator Clayton Eshleman describes:

> My apprenticeship, by the beginning of 1964, consisted of:
>
> > —Visits to Corman at the Muse, and a correspondence with a wide range of poets, including Jack Hirschman, Thomas Merton, Jerry Rothenberg, W.S. Merwin, Robert Kelly, Paul Blackburn, and Mary Ellen Solt.
> >
> > —Working on my own poems every morning, then after lunch motorcycling downtown to the Yorunomado coffee-shop where I translated Vallejo until suppertime.
> >
> > —After supper, I would walk the hill to a neighborhood coffee-shop and read for several hours.[31]

▸ Have students research and share stories in your discipline about well-known practitioners when they were students or apprentices. Painters, for example, may explore *The Letters of Vincent Van Gogh*[32] and explore the question, *how is being a student different from, or similar to, being an apprentice?*

▶ Explore the history of art as a longstanding cooperative phenomenon from Ancient Greece through the Renaissance to current times and how the roles and expectations of the apprentice have changed.

▶ Have students identify three living artists to whom they would like to apprentice themselves. Why did they pick those three artists? What would they hope to learn from their apprenticeships?

▶ Encourage students to embrace the freedom of being a beginner or an apprentice. No one is expecting to see masterful work! Use Shunryu Suzuki's famous line: "In the beginner's mind there are many possibilities; in the expert's mind there are few."[33] What are some advantages to being a beginner or an apprentice?

▶ Explore apprentice tropes in popular culture: *Star Wars*, *Kick-Ass*, *Kill Bill*, *The Karate Kid*, *Whiplash*, or *Kung Fu* (TV series). How are these helpful or unhelpful? Are they inspiring? Off-putting?

Tip 29

Grading Participation

Here is the scenario, probably not entirely unfamiliar to you as a faculty member in the arts: you block out time for independent work (open labs, studios, or writing workshops) so students can get caught up on their projects prior to critiques. Or perhaps you schedule time for thoughtful discussion on focused topics. As you plan these opportunities, your goal is to give students the time they need to do their best work. Yet only half of the students show up, and few actually come prepared to participate.

The disconnect here is in students' perceptions of what is actually important in the class. Their assumption is that everything that is important will count toward their grade. If the activity or assignment does not have a point value, it must be peripheral to the things that are important. If you value students' engagement—whether it's during open labs, critiques, or discussions—then you must communicate this value to them and consider assigning it a grade.

Here are a few ways you can communicate the importance of student engagement in opportunities they might otherwise view as peripheral or unimportant:

▸ Emphasize participation in all aspects of the course by contextualizing all opportunities within the overarching course goals. For example, explain to students how participating in focused discussions about art or artists will help them produce or improve their own work.

▸ Schedule or plan all opportunities to correspond with important milestones in the course. A major project critique, for example, might be preceded by open lab times and discussions of canonical artists or works in the weeks leading up to critique.

▸ Assess students' participation in specific situations, and be specific about how they should prepare. Students are more apt to participate appropriately if they know exactly what you expect of them.

▸ Don't *call* them "opportunities." Instead, use terms that reflect the importance of participation in the course. Some examples might be workshop time, studio time, or other terms that convey a specific purpose. Preparation for final critique or final revisions are also good suggestions for time otherwise labeled as free work.

FIGURE 19. *GREAT BLUE HERON IN FLIGHT* BY SARAH BARSNESS, SOLANO COMMUNITY COLLEGE, CA

Tip 30

Grading Discussions

Facilitating discussions can be one of the most inspiring parts of teaching in the arts. Because of the wide variety in content, history, viewpoints, and frequent media cross-pollination, our field presents many opportunities for critical thinking. Holding class discussions is one of the best ways for faculty to engage students and for students and faculty to explore new ideas.[34]

Discussions aren't always the easiest thing to manage, however. In any given class, there is great diversity in student willingness to jump in and add opinions to the mix. In fact, in the case of most students, making contributions takes some serious coaxing and finesse on the instructor's part. In addition, there is always potential for awkward silences, and conversation can easily veer off topic if the instructor does not exercise some control.

Teaching online also requires purposeful decisions about how to get your students involved in discussion threads. This environment lends itself to discussion stalemate as days sometimes pass between posts. The following are some proven techniques for grading that also pique student interest and involvement in discussions. These techniques work equally well for online and face-to-face class discussions.

▸ Set expectations early about tone, level of participation, and frequency of activity or engagement. Don't feel obliged to break moments of silence every time; students may benefit from these moments of thinking or reflection.

▸ Grade precisely. Use a rubric for grading discussion participation and make that rubric available to students on the first day of class. Explain your criteria clearly so students have an understanding of your expectations.

▸ Grade early. Students are encouraged by timely feedback on their performance on any task. A satisfactory grade on discussion participation goes a long way toward participation in future discussions.

▸ Craft your discussion questions so that they elicit real discussion. If you want to check basic knowledge or have students spit back an answer, incorporate other assessment methods, like quizzes, that may be more appropriate for that kind of measure.

▸ Use a rubric like the following sample participation rubric adapted from Palloff and Pratt:[35]

TABLE 1. SAMPLE PARTICIPATION RUBRIC

Weekly participation is graded pass/fail. You will need to earn at least 9 points each week to earn a passing participation grade.

CRITERIA	(3 POINTS)	(2 POINTS)	(1 POINT)	(0 POINTS)
Frequency of Engagement	Posts three times, distributed throughout the week.	Posts two times, but posts are limited to one day.	Posts one time.	Does not engage in discussion boards at all.
Initial Weekly Discussion Board Posts	Posts are well-developed with thought and preparation, and relate to key aspects of weekly topics.	Posts are well-developed, well thought through, and prepared.	Posts are adequate, but appear to be rushed in terms of thoughtfulness and preparation.	No posts.
Content Contribution	Posts a factually correct, reflective, and substantive contribution; advances discussion.	Posts information that is factually correct, but lacks full development of concept or thought.	Repeats statements already made, but does not add substantive information to the discussion.	Posts information that is off topic, incorrect, or irrelevant to the class.
Clarity & Mechanics	Contributes to discussion with clear, concise comments, formatted in an easy-to-read style, free of grammatical or spelling errors.	Contributes valuable information to the discussion, with minor clarity or mechanics errors.	Communicates in a friendly, courteous, and helpful manner, but with some errors in clarity or mechanics.	Posts contain multiple errors or are inappropriate to the discussion.
Follow-Up Discussion Posts	Demonstrates analysis of others' points; extends meaningful discussion by building on discussion.	Elaborates on discussion point(s) with further comments or observation.	Contributions are one-dimensional (for example, simply agrees or disagrees with classmates); does not enrich discussion.	Does not contribute to follow-up discussion.

FIGURE 20. *SLAB STUDY* BY NATASHA HAUGNES, ACADEMY OF ART UNIVERSITY, CA

Tip 31

Self-Assessment and Creative Process

One of the many skills artists must develop is the ability to engage critically with their own work. Such engagement allows students to deepen their ability to talk about art in general, understand their own process more deeply, and connect the dots between theory and practice. In *Self-Assessment at Alverno College*, it is noted that:

> How well students continue to develop as performing artists will depend to a great extent on how well they can learn to assess their own work. . . . As students develop in their ability to assess their own performance, they continue to improve their performance and also become aware of their own learning processes; in effect, they are learning how to learn.[36]

This is applicable to all artists, not just performing artists.

Self-assessment activities can help students develop a more nuanced self-awareness while also helping them see assessment as a tool that facilitates their own growth as artists. This sounds promising, but how can we get our students to self assess in meaningful, structured, and engaged ways? How can we ensure that reflecting on their own work is indeed a part of learning how to learn?

The following suggestions can help get you started:

▸ Ask students to grade themselves and to provide rationale based on the goals of the class. Discuss their grades and comments by comparing the grade and comments you provide for the same project. Is there any common ground? Did the student notice qualities that you missed?

▸ Ask students to write an obituary of their artistic work, imagining that it had been destroyed or lost forever. Use, as one example, Eleni Sikelianos's obituary of her father[37] to show how specificity of detail can evoke a kind of presence.

▸ Establish a vocabulary for self-assessment by providing a list of course- and discipline-relevant terms and concepts. Require students to use these terms when assessing their own work.

▸ Explore the relationship between self-assessment and revision. Ask students to articulate a plan of revision based on their self-assessment.

▸ Explore the relationship between self-assessment and art criticism. Ask students to write about their own work as though being exposed to it for the first time, imitating the style of an example of art criticism found in a magazine or online.

▸ Have students create a graphic map or other visual representation of their field on which they plot themselves to show where they think they are in relation to others. This map could include elements such as core skills, advanced skills, core knowledge and advanced knowledge, big questions that are being debated in their field as well as questions that have been resolved, and even types of activities that people in different places on the map engage in.

Tip 32

The Language of the Discipline

In addition to facilitating and nurturing our students' progress as artists, the grades we give—with supportive comments—can help teach the unique lexicon of our specific fields. But students will not absorb the specific language accidently. We need to be intentional about using signature terms and concepts of the discipline in all the ways we communicate to students. A good way to start is to create a list of select words and terms that align with the stated goals of the course. Integrate these terms into the syllabus, critiques, feedback, and comments that support the grades you give. A student's understanding of extensive discipline-specific language can thus be enhanced in a targeted, course-specific way. Assessment can then become a bridge to a dialogue about art history, art criticism, and art in general.

Consider the following ways to incorporate the language of the discipline into your course:

▸ At the beginning of the course, create and share a list of terms and concepts with the students. Tie the list to the learning goals for the course.

▶   Include the effective use and understanding of terms and concepts as one of the learning goals of the course.

▶   Require students to incorporate a minimum number of signature terms and concepts in self- and peer-assessment assignments.

▶   Use a wide variety of readings and articles (beyond the textbook) from your discipline to select the course's list of terms and concepts.

▶   Create assignments that invite students to apply the vocabulary in the classroom. In a painting class, for example, ask the students to complete a critique of their own work as though written by Paul Klee.

▶   Create assignments that target specific terms or concepts. In a creative writing class where metaphor is a focus, for example, have students only discuss the use of metaphor when critiquing each other's work.

▶   Assign group work where each member of the group is responsible for using a different term or concept in critiquing the same work of art.

▶   For vocabulary-intensive courses, consider giving short quizzes to do a focused check on students' understanding of key terms.

FIGURE 21. *BOOK 5 (FROM A COLLABORATION BETWEEN JAPAN AND THE UNITED STATES OF AMERICA)* BY RURIKO MIYAMOTO AND KATHERINE SANDNAS, HIBBING COMMUNITY COLLEGE, MN

Tip 33

Assessing Research

Research is as important in art as in any other field, but it looks different than it does in other academic departments. In the liberal arts and social sciences, doing research usually means doing a lot of reading. Documenting this research means creating a bibliography. In the sciences, research typically means conducting surveys or experiments. Documenting this work means publishing the study in a scholarly peer-reviewed journal or presenting the work at a conference.

Creative practitioners do research, too. Sometimes that research involves text-based sources, but more often it is observational or experiential. For example, a composer creating a song cycle about dogsledding might learn to mush, a sculptor exploring communication through texture might learn braille, a web designer might watch as users explore his website, an interior designer might visit all of the five-star hotel lobbies in San Francisco in preparation for her own design proposal, or a screenwriter could conduct observations on how people speak when they are anxious. We need to help students understand the importance of doing these kinds of research—these learning experiences, observations, interviews, and visits—and give them ways to document it.

What kind of research do you expect your students to do for specific projects? Once you have determined the answer to this question, create a course or department standard for documenting research.

Here are a few ways to make research visible, so that you can assess it objectively:

▸ Require a project research page, similar to a bibliography, to be turned in with each project. Give students examples of the types of research to include and a suggested format. For example:

• Gallery visit: name of gallery, date, length of visit.

• Conversation: name of person, position or title, date, length of conversation.

▸ Consider having students include two-sentence summaries of how each research point affected their process or project.

▸ Provide examples of what research looks like in your discipline to help students expand their concept of research and know what you are looking for.

▸ Just as liberal arts instructors teach students to assess their sources, artists can have students brainstorm a list of all possible types of research at the beginning of a project, then decide which interviews, experiences, museum visits, and so on will be the most worthwhile.

Tip 34

_____

Skills-Based Assignments

An enthusiastic first-year student posts her drawing for the first major critique of your figure drawing course. The drawing is bold, energetic, and confident. Your eye is instantly drawn to it in the sea of more tentative, labored drawings on the critique board. "Wow," you utter, as the sinking feeling takes hold: the drawing doesn't display varied line quality and proportion, the skills that you have spent the first four weeks teaching. _In addition_, the student produced this drawing in _marker rather than charcoal_, which is the required medium for the class. How do you respond? This is a skills-based course but your student seems to have either forgotten or ignored this fact.

Even in art school, skills-based courses or assignments with no creative component or goals may exist. Courses on software and classical drawing techniques, for example, may be very skills focused and offer little room for originality or discussion of creative process. While our syllabi may distinguish between skills and creative development, our students are often not as compartmentalized in their experience of art school. Students, especially first-year students, may perceive an F on a skills-based exercise as an overall assessment of their artistic talent or promise—as a message that they are not meant to be artists.

Contextualizing assessment in skills-based courses or assignments is crucial. Helping students to see how skills relate to the larger picture of being an artist can help them stay motivated. Here are a few ways to contextualize skills-based assignments:

▶ After critiquing a piece that is creative, but does not demonstrate the skills that the course focuses on, ask the student about the courses that *do* address creativity. (*Have you taken that course yet? You will thrive in that course.*)

▶ Have a just-for-fun group critique of a creative master's piece, using the rubric for one of your own assignments. A Picasso or Warhol piece would fail a classical figure drawing critique, for example. Use this activity to make the point that you are focusing on a specific set of skills that students will draw on and build on, but not use exclusively in their artistic futures.

▶ Develop a metaphor that helps you contextualize the work you are doing in your skills-based course. Some use a toolbox metaphor: having skills to draw accurate perspective, to code, or to create focal points are analogous to having rulers, paint brushes, and erasers in your toolbox. You don't use all of the tools for all of your projects, but you can draw on them when you need them. Frame the discussions you are having as in the toolbox (for focused skills-based work) or out of the toolbox (for larger contexts).

▶ Consider grading skills on a pass/no pass basis, and have students who do not pass redo their work until the work passes and the skill is acquired. This type of grading encourages mastery.

Tip 35

Creating Rubrics

Why did I get a C? What do I need to do to pull my grade up?

These are good questions, justifiably posed by many students. But answering them over and over can take a lot of instructor time. There are many varieties of Cs, and the feedback you offer to the student with the well-developed concept and unskilled implementation will differ significantly from the feedback you give the student with the undeveloped concept and perfectly crafted presentation.

Rubrics make project expectations transparent. Art students report having a better understanding of assignments and working harder when they have rubrics in their classes. Instructors report that rubrics save time and help them stay better focused on the goals of the assignment (see n38).

A basic rubric lists the criteria for a project in the left column. Descriptors offer descriptions of what the project looks like at various levels of achievement. Formats can vary, but a three-column rubric (see table 2) is a good format to start with.

TABLE 2. RUBRIC TEMPLATE AND SAMPLE

	EXCEEDS GOALS (A–B)	MEETS GOALS (C)	DOES NOT MEET GOALS (D–F)
Criterion #1	*descriptor*	*descriptor*	*descriptor*
Criterion #2	*descriptor*	*descriptor*	*descriptor*

SAMPLE RUBRIC FOR A SIMPLE EVENT POSTER:

	EXCEEDS GOALS (A–B)	MEETS GOALS (C)	DOES NOT MEET GOALS (D–F)
Concept	• *Concept is original and memorable, and it complements the event.*	• *Concept or theme is appropriate to the audience.* • *Concept fits the event.*	• *Poster feels like a list of event information.* • *No theme or concept is evident.* • *Concept is inappropriate for the target event.*
Hierarchy	• *Size, color, and contrast are used to create clear hierarchy.* • *Hierarchy moves the viewers' eyes intentionally through the design.*	• *The most important design element stands out and supports the intended communication of the poster.*	• *All elements appear equally important.* • *Unintended hierarchy confuses the message.*

If your department does not already have rubrics in place, create your own. Here is a short guide to getting started:

- Choose an important project in your course. Generally, one of the larger projects is a good place to start.

- List your criteria—generally no more than five. Criteria should be mutually exclusive, with as little overlap as possible between them. When listing criteria, the most important ones should be the skills you have been teaching and want to see evidence of in this project.

- Write descriptors by looking at some examples of student work, done in response to the project, and writing down the words that come to mind—words and phrases that you might say in critique— in the appropriate column. If you do not have authentic examples of student work to look at, do your best to imagine the range of work students will turn in.

- If you are having trouble figuring out how to list your criteria or otherwise getting started, ask a colleague for help. Ask your colleague to listen to you talk about the student work, help you organize the criteria, and take notes on your most common comments. These comments can become descriptors in your rubric.

- Once you have a rubric, test it out. Look at a piece of student work and note your gut-level reaction to it. What grade would you give the piece, without looking at the rubric? Then, fill out the rubric by highlighting all of the phrases that apply to the piece in question. Compare your initial reaction to the filled-out rubric. Does the distribution of your highlighted comments match the overall grade? Should the overall grade be adjusted? Should the rubric wording be adjusted? Do the highlighted phrases communicate the most important general feedback to the student? Adjust your rubric until you feel comfortable that the wording addresses the most important components of the project.

▶ Rubrics cannot cover all of the comments you would give to a student, but they can communicate the most common, most important comments that you find yourself making.

Tip 36

Using Rubrics

A well-written rubric can save you time when it comes to grading. Instead of writing the same comments repeatedly, you can just circle the preprinted comments that apply and then make individual comments more personalized. Using a rubric while grading also helps keep grading consistent.

While instructors usually feel a responsibility to offer substantial comments to support a final grade on a project, students are much more likely to pay attention to and act on formative feedback—the feedback given during process critiques—than to summative feedback or feedback that accompanies a final grade.

Rubrics can be especially helpful in formative critiques and other early phases of projects. Here are a few ways to incorporate rubrics into the early phases of projects:

- Hand out the rubric with the assignment to help reinforce the assignment parameters. Many students report that having the rubric at the outset of an assignment helps them understand the assignment parameters better.[38]

- Hand out the rubric as students are finishing their first drafts. If you think your students may be overwhelmed by your rubric, introduce it

FIGURE 22. *PASTURE II* BY MARY SWANN

later in the process. Beginning students, especially when they are exploring new media, should experiment without having to worry about assessment standards.

▶ Refer to the rubric in critiques—having the categories and descriptors on hand can help to focus a critique.

▶ Have students self assess using the rubric: they mark up the rubric and comment on their own work before turning it in to you.

▶ Use the rubric as a basis for peer critique.

▶ Have students create their own rubric before they see the one you have created. Compare the versions of the rubric to assess students' perceptions of the course's standards.

▶ Give feedback on first drafts by marking up a rubric, indicating where the student needs to improve. Have students hand in that rubric with their final versions of a project along with a short statement about how they addressed the feedback in the rubric.

FIGURE 23. *BEAR (TREES)* BY GARY HAWKINS, WARREN WILSON COLLEGE, NC

Tip 37

When to Introduce a Rubric

Will the rubric scare my students if I give it to them early? Or will it help them better understand my expectations? Will it squelch their creativity— or enhance it?

The answer to all of those questions is "Yes, sometimes."

In order to answer the question for your own class, you need to determine whether the students will perceive the rubric as a grid of judgments from an authority figure, or whether they will see it as a tool that helps clarify the expectations of the assignment and gives them more control over their learning. It relies on you knowing your students, their confidence level, their relationship to the creative process, the clarity of your assignments, the quality of your rubric, and how you integrate it into your teaching.

In general, art students whose instructors use rubrics want to see the rubrics early on, especially when they are accompanied by samples of previous student work, according to one large study.[39] The rubric clarifies the parameters—the nonnegotiables—for an assignment. So rather than spending energy and time trying to understand the expectations, a student can spend that effort creating. Many students even report that good rubrics enhance their creativity. It seems that they read the guidelines in the rubric as a clear set of creative constraints rather than judgments.

On the other hand, the authors have anecdotal evidence of rubrics squelching the energy and creativity in a classroom. At one university, drawing instructors who introduced rubrics on the first day of class to first-year students reported that students became fixated on the grids of language, and the joy drained out of their classes. Similarly, in a creativity workshop where participants were asked to make a greeting card and "have fun," we found that distributing a simple rubric to one subgroup invariably stifles that subgroup's perceived creativity and yields greeting cards that are much less interesting than non-rubric groups' cards.

▸   Introduce the rubric early to experienced students who have some confidence in the subject matter. They should see the rubric as a tool that helps them complete the work in your class.

▸   Introduce the rubric early if your students tend to have a lot of trouble understanding the assignment.

▸   Introduce the rubric in the middle phase of a project, without any numbers or grades attached to it, as a guideline when an assignment or project has an element of critique or peer-critique. Tell students that the rubric will be a guideline for their final grade on the project. This middle ground approach can support an instructor's effort to build confidence in the early phases of a project and also communicate transparent criteria for grading.

▸ When you first introduce a rubric, take time to provide an overview of what a rubric is, to provide examples and samples, and to clearly articulate how rubrics will or won't be used for grading in the course.

▸ Give the rubric to students at the last class meeting before a project is due for them to self assess and make final adjustments to their work.

▸ If you want to help clarify expectations, without overwhelming and intimidating students, introduce a simplified form of the rubric and lots of samples of previous student work for freshman projects.

▸ DON'T introduce a rubric if the goal of your lesson is to get students to engage in the early play stage of the creative process. Play should be exploratory and free of perceived monitors.

▸ DON'T hand out a rubric that contains lots of judgment language (e.g., immature, unprofessional, lazy, fabulous, mediocre). That rubric may help guide your grading, but sharing it with the students will not give them the sense of control that is at the heart of motivation.

Tip 38

Student-Generated Rubrics

Sometimes, in spite of our best efforts to empower and involve students, we still get the feeling that students are waiting to be told exactly what to do. We may be left wondering if the students have internalized any sense of what good work looks like in our discipline.

Student-generated rubrics are powerful tools for involving students in the teaching and learning process. They are a way of formally asking students: *What do you think quality looks like in this course or discipline?* Creating a rubric can give students a sense of control over their own learning and the assessment process. Watching students construct a rubric can also provide instructors with insight into what students are learning, or how they view their discipline.

While an instructor-generated rubric is a tool for communicating expectations and standards, a student-generated rubric serves as a snapshot of students' understanding and learning. Sometimes a student-generated rubric can provide the basis for an instructor's grading rubric, but in general, this is not the goal of having students create rubrics.

Student-generated rubrics used in the first week of class can be good diagnostic tools to help you analyze their areas for growth. Having students

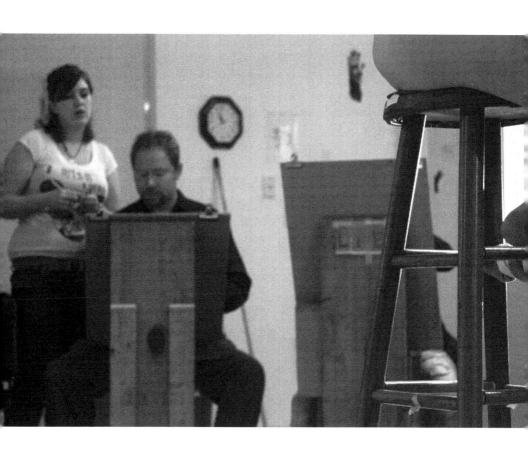

FIGURE 24. *UNTITLED* (FROM THE TEACHING AND LEARNING PROJECT) BY MARTIN SPRINGBORG, MINNESOTA STATE, MN

re-create the rubrics at the end of the semester also provides a sort of pre/post-test that shows how students' seeing or thinking has changed over the course of the semester. You can have students make rubrics as a way to check their understanding of a unit that has just been completed. A unit on typography, for example, may be followed up with the assignment to bring in examples of unacceptable, adequate, and exceptional typography along with written descriptions of each level. You can then assess whether they have internalized the main points of the unit.

Broad rubrics (e.g., those that distinguish between exceptional, adequate, and uninteresting films) can uncover students' ways of seeing their discipline, and can be helpful for courses that address these broad understandings (e.g., Introduction to Motion Pictures or Aesthetics of Motion Pictures). Students may not be expected to produce the work they are describing in their rubric, but they can clarify their evolving understandings of quality in the discipline. More focused rubrics can help you and your students home in on specific skills that you are teaching in your class. For those rubrics, the criteria will be closer to what the students actually can produce. Creating rubrics in this way helps students define the next step in their learning, and it helps them self assess.

Students who are completing final thesis projects or other individualized, self-directed projects may also benefit from creating a rubric for their own guidance and self-assessment. This rubric can help them articulate their own goals and communicate them to advisors.

Here are a few approaches to student-generated rubrics:

- Pose a big question or problem (e.g., name three to four criteria you look at when you critique motion pictures). Then have students generate categories or criteria in small groups. As a class, compare those criteria and agree on one main list of three to four criteria. Finally, have students fill in the descriptors in their groups and compare their rubrics to those generated from other groups.

- Have students create a rubric, then compare it to the one that you use, addressing the same set of skills or learning goals. This exercise should demonstrate that students already know a lot of what they need to know—that the criteria are not arbitrary.

- After a critique, have students create a rubric that reflects the standards or talking points that were discussed throughout the critique. *"After this critique and looking at all of your peers' work, can you make some generalizations about what the really strong work looks like? How about the adequate work? And what are the common pitfalls that we have seen come up in today's critique—the things that are to be avoided?"*

Tip 39

Rubrics for Peer and Self-Assessment

Well-intentioned instructors looking to involve students more in critique are sometimes disappointed by classroom peer critiques: "Their comments were so shallow—they did not seem to know what to say and seemed scared of offending each other." Rubrics can guide students through peer critique as well as self-assessment, transferring some of the responsibility and control to the students.

"Rubrics give students the power of access, to better understand expectations, to have a greater stake in their own learning," write Dannelle Stevens and Antonia Levi in their "Rubrics Manifesto" (see the Part II Supplementary Resources). As this quote suggests, the authors call for instructors to share control and power of education with students through rubrics—to draw back the curtain on our grading processes and judgments so that students can be participants, not followers, or worse, victims, of our processes.

In a classroom, when students assess each other and themselves, the instructor can build on what they have said—he or she can agree or disagree, expand on finer points, and coach students on *how* to get to the next level. This approach fosters independence and students' ability to self assess, which is so important to success in the art and design worlds. It also shifts the burden of work from the instructor—who is often scrambling to cover everything in a critique while students' attention wanders—to the students.

▸ Model using your rubrics before asking students to use them in peer critiques. Review the content of the rubrics, critique a piece together, and then have students mark up the rubrics, adding any important comments that might be missing. Have students compare marked up rubrics among themselves, then with you. Finally, address any points of strong disagreement. Agreement needn't be 100% on all points, but dramatic disagreements signal that a review of some content may be needed.

▸ Don't have students grade each other or calculate points for each other. Discussing the numbers or letters will likely detract from discussion of the criteria—the quality of the work. Keep the focus on the rubric criteria and descriptors.

▸ For skills-based work or other stand-alone work that does not require an oral presentation, divide students into groups of three. Have each group critique the pieces created by students in another group so that no one is participating in a discussion of their own project. The group discusses and fills out one rubric for each piece while the instructor circulates, listening in and offering guidance as needed.

► For work that involves an oral presentation, follow the same method as described in the previous point. When it comes time to fill out the rubric, have the artist do it for himself while the group fills theirs out. They may compare their assessments.

► Have students fill out rubrics for themselves and turn them in with every assignment or project.

► When you are grading and giving feedback, build on the self- and peer-completed rubrics and comments. Do not repeat what has already been said. Ground your own comments and assessment in students' input, clarifying where you agree and where you disagree, and filling in any points that are missing or that have been misunderstood.

Tip 40

Common Rubric Pitfalls

Sometimes instructors who are new to rubrics are hesitant to hand them out because they fear they have not perfected their rubrics. However, the only way to tell if your rubric is effective is to put it into use, either in a norming activity with a group of instructors (see tip 50), or in class with your students. It takes a while to get the wording on a rubric just right— sometimes it takes several semesters.

But you can check your rubric for some of the most common pitfalls before you share it with your students. Ask yourself the following questions as you examine your rubric:

- Have you avoided judgment words such as *good*, *nice*, *bad*, and *acceptable*? Including *good* in a descriptor in the "A–B" column of a rubric is redundant. Instead describe what *good* looks like for that particular assignment. Table 3 shows the transformation of one criterion from a rubric for an assignment in which students pitch an idea.

- Have you described the not passing category as objectively as possible? Imagine that you are highlighting those descriptors for a student who worked really hard, but has not yet mastered that criterion. Frame mistakes or deficits as stepping-stones to better work, as shown in table 4.

TABLE 3. AVOIDING JUDGMENT WORDS

BEFORE (WITH JUDGMENT WORDS):

	A–B	C	D–F
Visuals (slides)	Good visuals capture the audience's attention.	Adequate visuals.	Poor visuals.

AFTER:

	EXCEEDS GOALS (A–B)	MEETS GOALS (C)	DOES NOT MEET GOALS (D–F)
Visual presentation (slides)	Visuals complement and enhance the presentation through simple, original, and communicative images and consistent, clean design.	Visuals support the presentation through: • few, if any words • consistent layout • fonts and images that are readable from the back of the room.	Slides distract from the presentation due to one or more of the following: • too many words • visuals that distract from the main purpose of the presentation • clichéd choices of visuals • cluttered layout • lack of readability from the back of the presentation room.
Hierarchy	• Size, color, and contrast are used to create clear hierarchy. • Hierarchy moves the viewers' eyes intentionally through the design.	• The most important design element stands out and supports the intended communication of the poster.	• All elements appear equally important. • Unintended hierarchy confuses the message.

TABLE 4. OBJECTIVE DESCRIPTIONS

BEFORE (WITHOUT OBJECTIVE DESCRIPTIONS):

	A–B	C	D–F
Concept	*Concept for the ad reflects a keen creative mind. It is attention-grabbing.*	*Concept for the ad is okay.*	*Concept for the ad shows sloppy, lazy thinking.*

AFTER:

	A–B	C	D–F
Concept	*Concept is original and appropriate.*	*Concept is appropriate to the product being advertised, but not obvious.*	• *Concept is predictable—the one that most people would come up with first for this project.*

▸ If you find that you are repeating words in a rubric, figure out a more efficient way to lay it out. Too many words will overwhelm students, and they will not read rubrics if they are repetitive. Table 5 shows one example of this transformation.

TABLE 5. AVOIDING REPETITION

BEFORE (WITH UNNECESSARY REPETITION):

	A–B	C	D–F
Revision	*Student incorporates feedback on all drafts*	*Student incorporates feedback on most drafts*	*Student incorporates feedback on no drafts*

AFTER:

	A–B	C	D–F
Revision: Student incorporates feedback	*Always*	*Most of the time*	*Seldom to never*

Tip 41

_____

Structuring the Critique

Critique. This forum for constructive criticism from our colleagues and peers is at the heart of most arts and design courses. We can't work in a vacuum. We need to learn from others who are making new and exciting work, and we need to hear what our audience, peers, or colleagues think about our work.

The critique model has been a part of art instruction since the emergence of formal apprenticeships. It has become a signature pedagogy, a way of teaching that is specific to one discipline, for creative fields. When critique sessions work well in our classes, they result in great things—new ideas, new directions, and light bulb moments for our students. We see possibilities students had never before considered. When critique sessions don't work well, there are long, awkward silences; blank stares; or nervous, empty comments like "good job." We may do all the talking because our students won't or don't engage. Our students come out of these critique sessions still needing individual feedback and direction from us—not having received adequate input during the critique session.

In order to have successful critiques every time—those that yield those new ideas and aha! moments—we need to think through the critique process prior to running it. Too often, we conduct them as we

FIGURE 25. *ANN AND POLLY* BY STANLEY F. WITHE

participated in them as students—as open free-for-all comment sessions. Students in these scenarios do not readily lend constructive criticism to their peers, but instead give imprecise comments such as "I like it" or "it needs work." As instructors, we then devote precious critique time to clarifying the concept of constructive criticism instead of focusing adequate time and attention on actually critiquing.

We can avoid those unproductive or counterproductive critique sessions with a little preplanning and intentional structuring of the session. Think back to your most fruitful or inspiring critique sessions as a student or practicing artist. What was it that made them so productive? What happened that gave you the ideas you needed to take your work to the next stage of development? Think about what you want to accomplish with your classroom critique. What should your students gain? What should you gain in terms of assessing student progress and giving students feedback so they can take those critical next steps? Now, articulate those moments and ideas; simply list them on a sheet of paper. Those are your criteria for a successful classroom critique. Given these criteria, consider the following tips for replicating that ideal critique session:

▸ Consider the size of the critique group. What makes the most sense, given your ideal criteria? Would students (and you) gain more from a small-group, individual (peer-to-peer), or large-group setting? If you have a larger class, consider breaking the critique into smaller groups. If you have a smaller class, everyone may benefit from discussing work all together.

▶ Treat the critique as you would any activity or assignment and make clear learning objectives for your students. These objectives might include students learning or using new vocabulary relevant to the discipline. The objectives should include them providing their peers with constructive criticism and receiving direction for their own work—from their peers, as opposed to you alone. This will be especially helpful for new students or students new to the critique process.

▶ Consider how you will purposefully meet these learning objectives. For example, what kinds of comments or feedback meet the minimum criteria for constructive criticism? What vocabulary (of the medium, from units you've studied) do you need students to use during the critique session? In the early stages of a painting foundations course, you might emphasize the use of color, line, form, texture, and the like. Consider articulating the use of these terms in a rubric that you share with your students before the critique.

▶ To know whether your students received adequate direction in their own work and whether the critique session was successful for them, take some time immediately following the critique to have students write what they learned about their own work. Have them articulate their plans for next steps.

Tip 42

Critiquing in the Online Environment

Does the distance-learning environment change the way we assess student work? The short answer is no, it shouldn't. The longer, more accurate, and complicated answer is no, it shouldn't, . . . and yes, it does.

For all the online connectivity we have these days, those of us teaching online are often frustrated at the relative disconnect and ongoing challenge of developing a sense of community that we recognize as critical to our students' success. Stemming from that realization, perhaps the most challenging aspect of teaching online is conducting critique—a key step in the process of assessing student work in arts and design disciplines.

For those faculty who are new to teaching arts and design courses online, the first concern is that the real-time, give-and-take quality of critique will disappear in place of major delays and lots of typing. Thankfully, the set of tools available to online instructors has expanded and evolved at a rapid pace in recent years, and it continues to grow and change with new faculty needs and expectations. Various voice and annotation tools facilitate the sharing of visual work in a way that replicates key elements of face-to-face critique sessions. Students can assemble a portfolio, insert

first offering

road along the bottomlands
snow melt and still
jack-knifed truck in a ditch
when it comes she said there is nothing you can do
it's gonna take you
so many old wooden houses
grown over in wild vines the ground
a silver fire of mown corn
one day you will have to let go of everything
and what can help you
is it the wide fields the dark eyes of the deer
I have been awful things
I have been the light falling
over us the wing beat of vultures
of swans from the north
where the road crosses over the water

—Gillian Parrish

FIGURE 26. *FIRST OFFERING* BY GILLIAN PARRISH

audio comments, and use various annotation tools to draw viewers' attention to specific aspects of individual pieces. Their fellow students (and instructor) can, in turn, view the portfolio of work and add their own audio comments and markup. The give-and-take aspect of critique does not need to be replaced by boring text.

Consider the following tips for making online critiquing more effective:

- If you teach in an asynchronous online environment, use voice and annotation tools to conduct your critiques. Plan on this taking a few days to a week if you would have taken one class session to conduct a face-to-face critique.

- If you teach in a synchronous online environment, conduct one-on-one critiques using real-time conferencing tools that allow you to share images and talk to each other.

- Record your synchronous critique sessions and post the recordings in your Learning Management System (LMS). Ask students to meta-analyze their critique experience and either self-critique or peer-critique after watching the recording. This is something you can do perhaps more effectively online than you can do in traditional classrooms.

- Use peer review sheets to guide critiques. These are helpful in face-to-face courses, but crucial in online courses, where it can take longer to repair or refocus a discussion that isn't moving toward the outcomes that you want.

- Have students write short reflection papers after each critique to ensure that they have read and internalized the critique comments.

Tip 43

Peer Critique

One of our goals in arts courses is to help students give critical feedback on each other's work. However, if getting them to that point is not deliberate or well planned, students tend to avoid peer critique. Given the option, some students might sooner do anything else (like get a root canal).

Actually, it's not that difficult to get students to engage in peer critique if we introduce the process slowly and return to it often as a vital, necessary part of being an artist. As early as the first day of the semester is a good time to introduce the critique process—specifically peer critique—as a course goal. Returning to the process to model effective and constructive critique, as a foreign language instructor might immerse the class in the language being studied, will make students strong practitioners who are aware of the importance of peer critique postgraduation.

The obvious place to introduce and foster peer critique is in our regular critique sessions, where we lead students in giving constructive criticism. Simple, direct, and *specific* questions such as "What do you think about the use of depth of field in this photograph?" invite students to lend their voices to the discussion. Specific questions that focus students' comments on the objectives of the assignments help keep the critique productive and constructive. Inviting students' input more often as critique sessions continue throughout the semester tells them that their input is valuable to their classmates. Once you feel your students are ready to conduct peer critiques with little supervision, consider the following tips:

▸ Start peer critiques in smaller groups. It's easier for students to open up to a few peers vs. the entire class.

▸ Model effective constructive criticism in early critique sessions, when you are more directly in control of the process. For students who are new to critiquing, you might include a quick meta-discussion of the type of descriptive language and questions that are appropriate (*Have you thought about* _____? *When I see* _____, *it makes me think* _____.), as opposed to language that can put peers on the defensive (*You should* _____. *I don't like* _____.).

▸ Let go of your control over the critique process slowly and in deliberate phases—giving more control and more voice to students over time. As you offer more time for peer critique, make sure your involvement in the process is as a guide. Ask questions of your students, but limit what you add to the critique in terms of comments on work. Make your focus the students and their participation.

▸ Require student participation in peer critique and make it part of their overall project grade.

▸ Ask students specific questions to guide them through the process. These might look a lot like leading questions you would use to open any critique session. They will serve to set the structure for your students as they take control over the process. Questions should relate directly to your learning objectives for the critique session.

Tip 44

Art Directing vs. Critiquing

"I had been overly critiqued on my designs . . . it was just work now. It wasn't even fun anymore." [40] —Upper division undergraduate student

Art and design instructors come to the field of teaching from a variety of industries. Some, in their previous position of art director, oversaw the production of ad campaigns, games, films, or websites. They may have learned their skills working for another art director, or even taught junior designers as art directors themselves. Stepping into the role of art director can seem like an authentic, natural role to assume during a critique, but this may not be so helpful to students learning in the long run.

The art director's job is to ensure that the final product adheres to his or her aesthetic standards. Art directing is appropriate in some types of assignments and critiques. For example, when students are learning to use certain tools, following art director–like directions is a good way to show that they have the agility to manipulate all of the tools. Likewise, giving students specific constraints can help them to focus on specific skills. For example, allowing a specific color palette in early design assignments takes away the complication of choosing color and allows students to focus on other compositional elements. Art directing can arise in any arts discipline and will almost always result in work that looks or sounds really good. That can be encouraging for beginning-level students, even if they did not come up with the concept themselves.

But in assignments and critiques where the goal is creative development, students need to maintain ownership of the work and take responsibility for the decisions they make. Art directing robs them of this opportunity. Instructors need to remember that the intended outcome of the teaching work they are doing is *advancing student skills and knowledge,* not producing beautiful work.

To make sure you are not art directing your students, consider the following:

- Talk to colleagues and your program director to find out if the student work from your class is recognizable and distinct from other work in the department, and if so, why? Is it because of the content of the class? Or is it because you are imposing a particular style on your students?

- Develop an awareness of when you direct students to fix things and when you are grading based on the students making the requested fixes. Try replacing fix-it language with more objective statements and questions to find out whether the student knows how to proceed. For example, "Replace that script font with something newer like Noelan" will lead the student to dutifully search out Noelan and replace the font. But "That script font is overused and outdated. How can you find something fresher?" offers clear objective feedback and invites a discussion of *how* to get to the next step rather than what, exactly, to do.

▸ Ask authentic questions. "You can see how this brighter shade of red pops better, right?" is not really a question because the student knows the answer you are looking for ("*Yes, of course!*"), and they will obediently replace the red with the one you suggested. Try instead, "Let's look at some other shades and you can tell me which one you think pops more." Or, "How might you find a shade that works with the other colors but pops more?" These last two questions put more of the decision-making power in the student's hands.

Tip 45

Critique Journals

But that's not what you told me to do last *week!*

In spite of our best efforts to communicate clearly, the parties involved sometimes leave with very different memories or interpretations of what transpired in a critique. Your comment on a very minor detail (e.g., "A darker value in the background might help . . . ") might be the one thing that the student is able to act on immediately (and therefore the one thing that they remember), when in fact the piece you were critiquing had far bigger issues.

Critique journals are places for students to capture the main takeaways from critiques. They make students' understandings (or misunderstandings) visible, and can provide a useful record of students' progress on their learning paths over the course of a semester.

Critique journals can be digital or pen and paper. They can be highly structured or loose. The content is generated mostly by the student, but can also include comments from other students and from the instructor. You should not need to review them at the end of every critique, but students should make them available during all discussions with you. Consider how you will incorporate a critique log into the teaching and learning in your course. Here are a few approaches:

FIGURE 27. *WEEPING ADONIS* BY GERARD SANTIAGO, ACADEMY OF ART UNIVERSITY, CA

- Give students a chart with basic headings or questions that they should include in their journals after every critique. Examples include strong points, points to improve, other notes, and next steps.

- Assign different journal questions each week, in addition to the basic or standard questions you use. For example: How has your understanding of color changed in these first four weeks of the semester?

- Allow each student to take five minutes away from the main group immediately after their critique to capture their takeaways in their critique journal.

- Allow a student who is being critiqued to give their critique journal to a classmate to take notes for them. This allows the one being critiqued to focus on the discussion.

- Check the entries of students who are struggling before they leave class or during your next office hour to make sure they are leaving with a realistic, appropriate record of the critique and plan for work.

- Weekly detailed grading of critique journals could become cumbersome and may interfere with the students' ownership of the contents. Consider grading the weekly critique journals on a pass/no pass basis.

- Two or three times a semester, have students go back through their journals to see what patterns emerge. Have them state what lessons arise from those patterns. These papers can comprise part or all of the process component of your grade if you include one in your class.

▶ In one-on-one, or desk critiques, have students write the questions they have for you about their work in their critique journal. Have them leave the notebook open on their desk or a document open on their screen so that you can quickly scan the room to see who is ready for a critique. Similar critique readiness signals can be created in an online course.

Part II Supplementary Resources

Further reading on communicating goals

Ambrose, Susan A., Michael W. Bridges, Michele DiPietro, Marsha C.
  Lovett, and Marie K. Norman. *How Learning Works: Seven Research-Based Principles for Smart Teaching.* San Francisco: John Wiley &
  Sons, 2010.
An insightful and accessible guide to improving teaching in all disciplines.
The book references a wealth of compelling research to offer practical suggestions and guidance.

Bain, K. *What the Best College Teachers Do.* Cambridge, MA: Harvard
  University Press, 2004.
Bain's study of the "best college teachers," some of whom are in the arts,
yields a portrait of not only what the best college teachers do but also how
they think. We wholeheartedly recommend the entire book. Chapter 4
("What Do They Expect of Their Students?") in particular includes good
guidance for setting expectations for students and communicating these
expectations in a way that motivates.

Barbezat, Daniel P., and Mirabai Bush. *Contemplative Practices in Higher Education: Powerful Methods to Transform Teaching and Learning.* San Francisco: Jossey-Bass, 2013.
A groundbreaking book that clarifies the effectiveness of contemplative practices in higher education while providing practical examples of how to get started—whether or not the instructor has any prior experience with contemplative practices. Useful for all disciplines.

Barkley, Elizabeth. *Student Engagement Techniques: A Handbook for College Faculty.* San Francisco: Jossey-Bass, 2010.
You can find plenty of easy-to-implement techniques to engage students in their learning in this book. The chapters on and strategies for building community, self-assessment, synthesis, and creative thinking are particularly pertinent to faculty in the arts.

Cranton, Patricia. *Understanding and Promoting Transformative Learning: A Guide for Educators of Adults.* San Francisco: Jossey-Bass, 1994.
This is a comprehensive resource for transformational learning strategies with fresh insights into the transformative journey of the educator.

Lakey, George. *Facilitating Group Learning: Strategies for Success with Diverse Adult Learners.* San Francisco: Jossey-Bass, 2010.
Lakey presents a coherent overview of group learning in the context of diversity and difference, with a wealth of guidance about how to turn diversity and difference in your classroom into a strength.

McKeachie, Wilbert, and Marilla Svinicki. *McKeachie's Teaching Tips.*
    Boston: Cengage Learning, 2014.
The bible of instructional guidance for higher education, McKeachie's timeless book is full of immediately usable tips for beginning and experienced faculty who wish to improve student learning. See Chapter 7, "Assessing, Testing, and Evaluating: Grading is Not the Most Important Function," and Chapter 10, "Assigning Grades: What Do They Mean?"

Simkins, Scott, and Mark Maier. *Just-in-Time Teaching: Across the
    Disciplines, Across the Academy.* Sterling, VA: Stylus Publishing, 2010.
A comprehensive guide to the pedagogical practice known as Just-in-Time Teaching (JiTT).

Steele, Claude M. *Whistling Vivaldi: How Stereotypes Affect Us and What
    We Can Do.* New York: W. W. Norton, 2011.
Claude Steele's research on stereotype threat provides insight into why students from nondominant cultures drop out of school at a higher rate than those from nondominant cultures. He also provides us with tools to potentially mitigate this difference.

Further reading on creative process

Bayles, David, and Ted Orland. *Art & Fear: Observations on the Perils (and
    Rewards) of Artmaking.* Santa Cruz, CA: Image Continuum, 1993.
This is an encouraging and conversational book, by artists, about making art.

Cain, Susan. "The Rise of the New Groupthink." *New York Times*,
    January 13, 2012.
This article provides an analysis of the importance of working solo and an
expanded discussion of the history and pitfalls of the group brainstorming
session.

Davis, Barbara Gross. *Tools for Teaching.* 2nd ed. San Francisco: Jossey-
    Bass, 2009.
This book is a universal guide to teaching in higher education, no matter
the discipline. Davis addresses topics from course preparation to finishing
the semester.

Eshleman, Clayton. *Novices: A Study of Poetic Apprenticeship.* Los Angeles:
    Mercer & Aitchison, 1989.
A deep dive into the psychology of apprenticeship: inspiring and
thought-provoking for the artist of any stripe.

Haugnes, Natasha, Hoag Holmgren, and Martin Springborg. "What
    Educational Developers Need to Know about Faculty-Artists in the
    Academy." *To Improve the Academy* 31, no. 1 (2012): 55–68.
Meaningful Grading authors collaborated on this article in response to
questions from fellow educational developers about communicating with
faculty artists.

Lehrer, Jonah. "The Eureka Hunt." *New Yorker*, July 28, 2008, 40–45.
This article provides an in-depth look at how aha! moments occur.

Pallasmaa, Juhani. *The Thinking Hand: Existential and Embodied Wisdom in Architecture*. Chichester: Wiley, 2009.
Written by a distinguished Finnish architect and architectural thinker, this is a fascinating reconsideration of the role and significance of architecture and a rallying cry for the reunion of body, mind, and art.

Pappano, Laura. "Learning to Think Differently." *New York Times*, February 9, 2014, Education Life.
This article includes a number of ideas for helping students embrace failure as part of the creative process.

Ross, Orna. "The Seven Stages of Creativity: Week 2 Incubation." *Writing.ie.*, accessed April 24, 2017, https://www.writing.ie/resources/the-seven-stages-of-creativity-week-2-incubation/.
Ross's article stresses the importance of incubation and gives some concrete ideas about how to incorporate this stage into one's own writing process.

Sawyer, R. Keith. "Enhancing Creative Incubation." *Psychology Today*, April 19, 2013.
Sawyer's article gives a succinct overview of the importance of incubation and play, especially in preparing our brains for moments of insight.

Sawyer, R. Keith. *Explaining Creativity: The Science of Human Innovation.* New
York: Oxford University Press, 2012.
This book provides the most comprehensive, up-to-date survey of research
in creativity that we have found. It is well written but dense, suitable for a
graduate course in the psychology of creativity. Pages 91–92 provide a
thorough overview of the eight steps of creativity. Readers looking for the
general audience version of these same steps should look at Sawyer's more
popular book *Zigzag: The Surprising Path to Constant Creativity* (San Francisco:
Jossey-Bass, 2013).

Van Gogh, Vincent. *The Complete Letters of Vincent Van Gogh.* Edited by
Ronald de Leeuw. Translated by Arnold J. Pomerans. Reprint, Boston:
Bullfinch Press, 1958.
A moving and inspiring account of a major artist's development and
self-knowledge as an artist.

Further reading on rubrics

Brookhart, Susan M. *How to Create and Use Rubrics for Formative Assessment
and Grading.* Alexandria, VA: ASCD, 2013.
This is a very practical book, full of ideas for creating rubrics as well as incorporating them into teaching and learning.

Haugnes, Natasha, and Jennifer L. Russell. "Don't Box Me In: Rubrics for Artists and Designers." *To Improve the Academy* 35, no. 2 (2016): 249–83.
This article describes a rubric creation process that was grounded in teaching and learning in art and design classrooms, and the follow-up study that assessed the students' and instructors' perceptions of rubric effectiveness.

Stevens, Dannelle D., and Antonia Levi. *Introduction to Rubrics: An Assessment Tool to Save Grading Time, Convey Effective Feedback and Promote Student Learning.* Sterling, VA: Stylus Publishing, 2013.
Introduction to Rubrics is a valuable, accessible guide to rubrics, with many examples, and an impassioned "Rubrics Manifesto."

Further reading on critiquing

Barrett, Terry. *Criticizing Photographs: An Introduction to Understanding Images.* New York: McGraw-Hill, 2011.
One of the earliest texts on the subject of critique in photography courses, many of the approaches outlined in *Criticizing Photographs* are easily adaptable to any fine or studio art course.

Palloff, Rena, and Keith Pratt. *Assessing the Online Learner: Resources and Strategies for Faculty.* San Francisco: Jossey-Bass, 2009.
This book is a helpful and lasting guide to all online instructors. Contents include examples for grading student engagement in online courses as well as ideas for course and program evaluation.

FIGURE 28. *TWO DEER* BY MARY SWANN

PART III

Post-semester

Reflecting on a completed semester is crucial to establishing and improving meaningful grading practices.

FIGURE 29. *CHARACTER* BY HA HOY HOANG, ACADEMY OF ART UNIVERSITY, CA

Tip 46

Requesting Feedback on Your Grading

Instructors can feel lost when trying to determine the accuracy and impact of grades as the semester progresses. Unless a student complains about or petitions for a higher grade, there will likely be little dialogue regarding the significance and meaning of grades. Intentionally requesting feedback on grading can improve the assessment of student work and get students talking about their work, their process, the course, the material, and the course goals. It also demonstrates to students that you value their input, which helps communicate the importance of student engagement.[41] Moreover, there is abundant evidence that student feedback can be both meaningful and relevant.[42]

It can also be helpful to seek feedback on your own grading from faculty colleagues. This has added benefits such as expanding one's professional network (especially when reaching out to faculty in other departments) and identifying colleagues who can offer support, collaborations, or mentoring in other areas.

▸   Be clear from the beginning of the semester that you will solicit feedback on grades. Clarify how and when the feedback will be collected as well as how you will respond to the feedback. Ask, for example, "Do you think the grade is fair? If you do not think the grade is fair, please indicate what you think the grade should have been, and why. Please refer to the same rubric I used to grade your work." Follow up by email or meet individually with students as needed for further discussion.

▸ Students should understand that your request for feedback on grades will not automatically result in a grade change. The point of requesting feedback, and then discussing that feedback with students, is for students to gain a more nuanced understanding of their own work *as well as* to help the instructor be more effective with grading.

▸ Brief weekly or monthly requests for feedback might include: "Do you feel that the grading in this course is helpful in understanding your own work or your own process? How might it be more helpful?"

▸ Adopt the do-it-yourself (DIY) approach to seeking feedback where you create your own feedback tool based on the unique needs of you and your course. There's no need to use a formal, pre-made instrument.[43]

▸ Require students to respond to at least two requests for feedback on grades.

▸ When seeking feedback on grading from colleagues, it can be helpful to share a sample of anonymous student work and ask how they would have graded it. Offer to reciprocate and meet occasionally to discuss grading.

Tip 47

Post-semester Community: Moving Beyond Assessment

An arts course is a kind of intentional microcommunity where creativity and safe personal exploration are primary values—for the instructor as well as the students. When the semester ends, students can long for the supportive and inspiring qualities of the community to continue. The instructor might also long for this, but also perhaps for a community of peers with whom she or he can compare notes and commiserate on shared challenges of instruction. Of course, BFA and MFA programs are larger intentional communities of faculty and students that last considerably longer than a semester, and students often have the same professor several times with many of the same students. But each course has its own unique group personality and sense of cohesion. Some classes can develop a family-like intimacy by the end of the semester, while others might not. Accordingly, some class communities are more amenable to continuing in some form than others.

Post-semester communities often naturally manifest where people stay in touch and continue to share their work long after the semester—or program—ends. While these relationships are valuable, and perhaps even crucial, they tend to be exclusive and defined by friendship alone. A more inclusive post-semester community, where more of the class is included, may retain more of the dynamics that made the class worth continuing in the first place: honest critique, healthy competition, and inspiring discussion. Discussing post-semester options with your students can help affirm that the class is not ultimately about static grades. It's about community and growing together as artists.

► Offer opportunities to the entire class, such as getting together for lunch or coffee once a month or once per week. This can be included in the syllabus or mentioned at the beginning of the semester. It should be clear that it's optional and will happen only if the class desires it.

► Be realistic in setting expectations, and let the post-semester community live out its natural life. It may be short lived or not happen at all.

► Seek out colleagues who might be interested in meeting informally on a regular basis for mutual support.

► Set up a social media group to stay connected.

► Be mindful of professional boundaries, and choose meeting places that are inviting to all.

► Students should be allowed to come and go as they please with no penalties or requirements. Likewise, the group should be open to new students joining from other classes. It may not be feasible or desirable to have more than one ongoing post-semester community.

▸ Post-semester communities can form publishing cooperatives, theatre troupes, art galleries, or music ensembles. Be open to possibilities.

▸ Consider starting a formal club at your institution where students can take part in rotating leadership roles (president, community outreach, marketing, etc.).

Tip 48

Reflecting and Planning for Next Semester

The end of a semester is a valuable time to capture reflections and information that can help you plan future courses. Examining the just-finished semester through the lens of your grading and feedback can lead to improvements in every aspect of teaching, not just grading practices. Take notes as you go through the following process:

▸ Start by reviewing your goals for the course. Then look at your final grades and consider the students individually. How well do the grades reflect your gut feeling about how well each student met the goals of the course? Are your grades measuring what you intend them to measure?

▸ Think back through your critiques. Did you meet the goals of your critiques? Did students implement the feedback that they received in critique? How did they engage in the process?

▸ How was the process of grading for you and your students? Were you confident in the grades you entered for most projects? Did students understand the meaning behind the grades, or did they seem confused?

When you identify an aspect of grading or feedback that you think could be improved, consider the whole ecosystem of your course as you plan changes for the following semester. Sometimes the issue is that the percentage of a certain project needs to be boosted in your calculation of the grade or the criteria on a rubric need to be reworked. But more often, there are other adjustments that can be put into place. Consider some of the following ways a course might be reworked as a result of identifying issues with the grading and feedback process:

▸ Course learning outcomes may need adjustment. If your students have not adequately met the outcomes, but have made tremendous progress in other ways, you or your director may need to reword the outcomes to more accurately reflect what you are actually teaching.

▸ Assignments may need to be reworked to elicit more of the target skills. This is often the case if you find yourself saying, "I know the students learned it, even if you can't see it in their projects."

▸ More opportunities for students to revise work need to be built in if students do not seem to be applying feedback. There should be some accountability in the grading criteria for incorporating feedback.

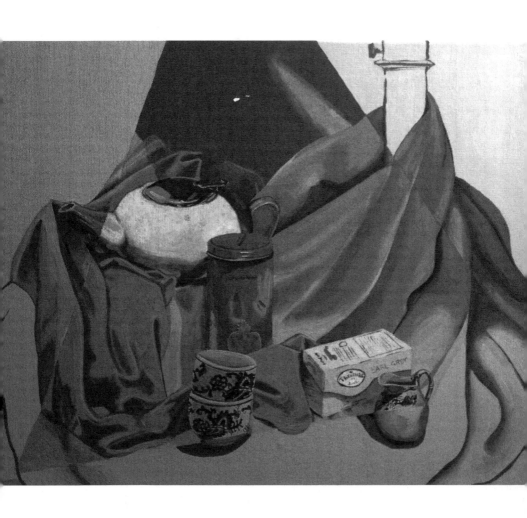

FIGURE 30. *STILL LIFE WITH TEA* BY SAMI TUTONE

Tip 49

End-of-Semester Evaluations

End-of-semester evaluations of our courses can provide valuable insights into student learning, appropriateness of workload, grading, and teaching methodologies. However, it's often unclear how to benefit from these insights and translate them into improved teaching and student learning. Student evaluations can be influenced by factors such as gender and ethnicity, which have nothing to do with teaching.[44] In order to get the most out of these evaluations, be prepared to weed out the unhelpful comments (on wardrobe or hair, for example) and focus on the ones that sincerely address your teaching and course. Ideally, end-of-semester evaluations are part of your ongoing course design and redesign process as well as your continuing professional development as an instructor.

The following are suggestions for getting the most benefit from your end-of-semester evaluations. For more on how to draft and solicit your own student evaluations of teaching, as well as the benefits and short-comings of mandated survey instruments, see tip 14, "Soliciting Feedback."

▸ Let students know that you value their evaluative input and will take their suggestions and comments seriously.

- ▸ Read the evaluations as soon as possible after receiving them. This will give you time to reflect on and process the information with the course still fresh in mind.

- ▸ Try to identify trends or patterns in student comments and responses. Also look for patterns among evaluations for other classes you might be teaching. Do certain comments or responses recur semester after semester or from course to course?

- ▸ Be sure to acknowledge and take into account what worked well in your course.

- ▸ Review your syllabus, learning goals, and course design materials in light of the evaluations; how might they be adjusted and improved? Begin redesigning courses, revisiting learning goals, and revising syllabi as soon as possible.

- ▸ Consult with a colleague or an educational developer to devise strategies for improvement based on evaluations.

- ▸ Archive your evaluations and look for evidence of improvement (or not) over time.

Tip 50

Norming Your Grades

"Take Jake's class if you want an easy A!"

"Really tough. I hardly slept that semester, but I learned a ton in Christine's class."

Discussions of instructors' grading processes abound on instructor rating websites or social media sites associated with your institution. Consistent grading practices communicate to students that your course—and hopefully the entire program—is cohesive and structured, leading them to a meaningful degree, not just through a series of personality-driven classes.

Gathering with colleagues to norm your grading is an excellent investment in your own teaching as well as in the department's consistency. At its core, a norming meeting is simply three things: instructors from your course or related courses + a stack of student work to look at + time. It can be very focused and specific to one course. If a rubric or other grading tool is standardized across all sections of a course, you should practice filling out the rubric in response to a piece and compare assessments to ensure that everyone is interpreting the rubric and grading in the same way.

A norming meeting can also be very helpful across programs or departments where there are no shared assessment tools. In these cases, the norming might just begin with a ballpark grade, with each instructor listing the top two to three points that they would give for feedback.

Norming meetings almost always result in instructors having more confidence in their grading and better focus on the course expectations. Students get more consistent feedback when teachers are normed, and teachers can assess work more efficiently and confidently when they know their judgment is in line with that of their colleagues. Faculty who teach subsequent courses can be confident in their expectations of students who are advancing into their classes. Program directors and department chairs are also able to field questions or concerns from students when they are confident the teachers are normed for the course in question. And discussions at norming sessions may also lead to improvements in assignments or rebalancing of expectations.

Below is a step-by-step guide on how to structure a norming meeting to ensure that you meet the goal of clarifying and aligning expectations—determining what constitutes passing work in a specific course (or at the end of a specific program). Make sure to check with your department chair before organizing such activities.

1. Gather up to five instructors from one course, or from a series of courses. Assemble several examples of student work from one assignment. Give yourselves about ninety minutes.

2. Review the assignment, if any of the instructors are not familiar with it.

3. Introduce the rubric (or other grading tool), if there is one. Acknowledge whether the rubric is set in stone, open for revision, or in need of an overhaul.

4. Focus on the "big buckets" to begin with, such as passing vs. not passing work and passing vs. exceptional work. It is much easier to reach agreement on large categorizations than on the distinctions between B and B-, for example.

5. Show one or two pieces of work and have the attendees grade them silently and individually, making notes about why they would assign their chosen grade and questions that come up. If the goal is to make sure that a rubric is usable, they should fill out the rubric. If the goal is a more general alignment of grading, then a grade and comments are sufficient.

6. Reveal your grades and rationale. This can be done anonymously (by voting electronically or handing in paper ballots, if you think it would be more open and honest). If you are conducting a norming meeting like this online, polling tools can be very useful for this phase of the meeting.

7. Discuss and compare assessments.

8. Keep the focus on the particular course expectations. Be careful not to let discussions veer into the abstract question of "what

makes good art?" Instead, focus on: What does acceptable specific performance (e.g., exposure, use of color, pronunciation, writing) look like for this assignment, at this level? It is helpful to have someone in the norming session who has the authority to answer questions and make decisions about how important a particular skill is in a particular course. If no one is available, you can compile a list of questions for a department chair to address in a subsequent meeting.

9. Repeat steps 5–8 until you and your colleagues are in agreement at least 75% of the time.

Part III Supplementary Resources

Further reading on post-semester work

Angelo, Thomas A., and K. Patricia Cross, *Classroom Assessment Techniques: A Handbook for College Teachers*. San Francisco: Jossey-Bass, 1993.

This is the original bible for "CATS," or classroom assessment techniques, which are practical, easy-to-implement activities that help instructors find out how well students are learning.

Chase, David, Jill L. Ferguson, and J. Joseph Hoey. *Assessment in Creative Disciplines: Quantifying and Qualifying the Aesthetic*. Champaign, Common Ground Publishing, 2014.

This comprehensive overview of theory and research in creative discipline assessment is useful for instructors looking for theoretical grounding for their practice. It also provides many useful case studies of program level assessment from art and design programs.

Davis, Barbara Gross. *Tools for Teaching*. 2nd ed. San Francisco: Jossey-Bass, 2009.

This book is a universal guide to teaching in higher education, no matter the discipline. Davis addresses topics from course preparation to finishing the semester.

"Student Evaluations of Teaching," Center for Teaching: Vanderbilt University, accessed February 12, 2017, https://cft.vanderbilt. edu//cft/guides-sub-pages/student-evaluations/#tips.

The section titled "Summaries of Research on Student Evaluations" contains succinct, up-to-date overviews of research on topics within this area.

Doyle, Terry. *Helping Students Learn in a Learner-Centered Environment.* Sterling, VA: Stylus Publishing, 2008.

This book casts the entire arc of the faculty career as an adventure of continual learning and development. This is an inspiring and helpful resource for the entire journey, from beginning faculty member to senior mentor.

Kuh, George, Jillian Kinzie, John H. Schuh, Elizabeth J. Whitt, and Associates. *Student Success in College: Creating Conditions That Matter.* San Francisco: Jossey-Bass, 2005.

This book advises faculty on promoting student success via lessons learned from the Documenting Effective Educational Practice (DEEP) project.

McKeachie, Wilbert, and Marilla Svinicki. *McKeachie's Teaching Tips.* Boston: Cengage Learning, 2014.

The bible of instructional guidance for higher education, McKeachie's timeless book is full of immediately usable tips for beginning and experienced faculty who wish to improve student learning. See Chapter 7, "Assessing, Testing, and Evaluating: Grading is Not the Most Important Function," and Chapter 10, "Assigning Grades: What Do They Mean?"

Rand, Glenn, and Richard Zakia. *Teaching Photography: Tools for the Imaging Educator*. Burlington, MA: Focal Press, 2006.

Although written specifically for photography instructors in higher education, much of this book's insight on matters from pre- to post-semester are easily adaptable to any creative discipline.

Weimer, Maryellen. *Inspired College Teaching*. San Francisco: Jossey-Bass, 2010.

An insightful guide to ongoing faculty professional development at any career stage. Topics cover end-of-course ratings, colleagues as collaborators, and reflection on teaching.

Acknowledgements

We would like to thank and acknowledge the many people and organizations who supported and contributed to the evolution of this book. All work is a collaboration on some level, and this book is no exception. This project began several years ago in the midst of our work as instructors and educational developers in art, design, and creative writing, grappling with many of the challenges we explore in this book at three very different postsecondary institutions. There was an emerging observation that we were not alone; many of our colleagues also wrestled with these issues—often year after year, and often without formal support.

So a big thank you to our educational development and faculty artist colleagues, past and present, who helped us see the light: the faculty and office of Faculty Development at the Academy of Art University (Vanessa Spang, Jennifer Russell, Molly Flanagan, Tony Albert, Sarah Sherwood, James Wu, and Marian Shaffner); the students and faculty in the Creative Writing Program, and the staff in the Graduate Teacher Program at University of Colorado at Boulder (especially Laura Border and Andy MacDonald); faculty and staff within the Minnesota State system of colleges and universities (especially Jake Jacobson and Lynda Milne). We also recognize our many inspiring colleagues in the POD Network in Higher Education, an organization committed to advancing the research and practice of educational development in higher education, who continue to lead the way in our profession.

Finally, we would like to thank the artists who contributed work to illuminate the pages of this manuscript: Sarah Barsness, Samantha Cohran, Robin Eschner, Gary Hawkins, Ha Hoy Hoang, Soren Holmgren, Ruriko Miyamoto, Gloria Oliver, Gillian Parrish, Katherine Sandnas, Gerard Santiago, Beth Sousa, Mary Swann, Aimee Binh Yen Truong, Sami Tutone, and Stanley F. Withe.

Notes

1. Mark Edmundson, *Literature Against Philosophy, Plato to Derrida: A Defence of Poetry* (Cambridge: Cambridge University Press, 1995), 7.
2. Dan C. Lortie, *Schoolteacher: A Sociological Study* (Chicago: University of Chicago Press, 2002).
3. Stuart E. Dreyfus and Hubert L. Dreyfus, "A Five-Stage Model of the Mental Activities Involved in Directed Skill Acquisition," *Operations Research Center, UC Berkeley*, (February 1980): http://www.dtic.mil/cgi-bin/ GetTRDoc?AD=ADA084551&Location=U2&doc=GetTRDoc.pdf.
4. K. Anders Ericsson, Ralf T. Krampe, and Clemens Tesch-Römer, "The Role of Deliberate Practice in the Acquisition of Expert Performance," *Psychological Review* 100, no. 3 (1993): 363.
5. Leora Baron-Nixon and Irene Hecht, *Connecting Non Full-Time Faculty to Institutional Mission: A Guidebook for College/University Administrators and Faculty Developers* (Sterling, VA: Stylus Publishing, 2007).
6. L. Dee Fink, *Creating Significant Learning Experiences: An Integrated Approach to Designing College Courses* (San Francisco: Jossey-Bass, 2013), 82-85.
7. Mary-Ann Winkelmes, David E. Copeland, Ed Jorgensen, Alison Sloat, Anna Smedley, Peter Pizor, Katharine Johnson, and Sharon Jalene, "Benefits (some unexpected) of Transparently Designed Assignments," *The National Teaching & Learning Forum* 24, no. 4 (2015): 4–7, https://doi.org/10.1002/ntlf.30029.
8. Thomas A. Angelo and K. Patricia Cross, *Classroom Assessment Techniques: A Handbook for College Teachers* (San Francisco: Jossey-Bass, 1993).
9. Deborah A. G. Drabick, Robert Weisberg, Luci Paul, and Jennifer L. Bubier, "Keeping It Short and Sweet: Brief, Ungraded Writing Assignments Facilitate Learning," *Teaching of Psychology* 34, no. 3 (2007): 172–76, https://doi.org/10.1080/00986280701498558.
10. Eric Booth, *The Music Teaching Artist's Bible: Becoming a Virtuoso Educator* (Oxford: Oxford University Press, 2009), 80.

11. Alyssa Friend Wise and Kevin O'Neill, "Beyond More Versus Less: A Reframing of the Debate on Instructional Guidance," in *Constructivist Instruction: Success or Failure?*, ed. Sigmund Tobias and Thomas M. Duffy. (New York: Routledge/Taylor & Francis Group, 2009), 82–105.

12. R. Reingold, R. Rimor, and A. Kalay, "Instructor's Scaffolding in Support of Student's Metacognition through a Teacher Education Online Course: A Case Study," *Journal of Interactive Online Learning* 7, no. 2 (2008): 139–151.

13. Philip Stark, "What Exactly Do Student Evaluations Measure?," *The Berkeley Blog*, October 24, 2013, http://blogs.berkeley.edu/2013/10/21/what-exactly-do-student-evaluations-measure/.

14. B. S. Bloom, "Mastery Learning," in *Mastery Learning: Theory and Practice*, ed. James H. Block. (New York: Holt, Rinehart and Winston, 1971).

15. Rhett McDaniel, "Student Evaluations of Teaching," Center for Teaching: Vanderbilt University, accessed April 27, 2017, https://cft.vanderbilt.edu/guides-sub-pages/student-evaluations/.

16. Susan A. Ambrose, Michael W. Bridges, Michele DiPietro, Marsha C. Lovett, and Marie K. Norman, *How Learning Works: Seven Research-Based Principles for Smart Teaching* (San Francisco: John Wiley & Sons, 2010), 170–187.

17. Erika A. Patall, Harris Cooper, and Jorgianne Civey Robinson, "The Effects of Choice on Intrinsic Motivation and Related Outcomes: A Meta-analysis of Research Findings," *Psychological Bulletin* 134, no. 2 (April 2008): 270–300.

18. Sheena S. Iyengar and Mark R. Lepper, "When Choice Is Demotivating: Can One Desire Too Much of a Good Thing?," *Journal of Personality and Social Psychology* 79, no. 6 (2000): 995–1006.

19. R. Keith Sawyer, *Explaining Creativity: The Science of Human Innovation* (Oxford: Oxford University Press, 2012), 88–90.

20. Sawyer, *Explaining Creativity*, 91–93.

21. Sawyer, *Explaining Creativity*, 235.

22. Sawyer, *Explaining Creativity*, 23.

23. Sawyer, *Explaining Creativity*, 100.

24. Paul Virilio, *Art and Fear* (Santa Cruz, CA: Image Continuum, 2010), 29.

25. Laura Pappano, "Learning to Think Differently," *New York Times*, February 9, 2014, Education Life.

26. Derek Thompson, "Inside Google's Moonshot Factory," *The Atlantic Monthly* 320, no. 4 (2017): 71.

27. Shauna L. Shapiro, Kirk Warren Brown, and John A. Astin, "Toward the Integration of Meditation into Higher Education: A Review of Research," *The Center for Contemplative Mind in Society* (2008), http://www. contemplative-mind. org/admin/wp-content/uploads/2012/09/MedandHigherEd.pdf.

28. Juhani Pallasmaa, *The Thinking Hand: Existential and Embodied Wisdom in Architecture* (Chichester: Wiley, 2009), 19.

29. Rainer Maria Rilke, *Letters to a Young Poet,* trans. Stephen Mitchell (Boston: Shambala, 1993), 49–50.

30. Cay Lang, *Taking the Leap: Building a Career as a Visual Artist* (San Francisco: Chronicle Books, 1998), 81–83.

31. Clayton Eshleman, *Novices: A Study of Poetic Apprenticeship* (Los Angeles: Mercer & Aitchison, 1989), 68.

32. Vincent Van Gogh, *The Complete Letters of Vincent Van Gogh.* Edited by Ronald de Leeuw. Translated by Arnold J. Pomerans. Reprint (Boston: Bullfinch Press, 1958).

33. Shunryu Suzuki, *Zen Mind, Beginner's Mind* (New York: Weatherhill, Inc., 1990), 21.

34. Barbara Gross Davis, *Tools for Teaching* (San Francisco: John Wiley & Sons, 2009), 63.

35. Rena M. Palloff and Keith Pratt, *Assessing the Online Learner: Resources and Strategies for Faculty* (San Francisco: John Wiley & Sons, 2008), 14: 29–30.

36. Alverno College Faculty and Georgine Loacker, *Self Assessment at Alverno College* (Milwaukee: Alverno College Institute, 2000), 121.

37. Eleni Sikelianos, *The Book of Jon* (San Francisco: City Lights Books, 2004), 109–110.

38. Natasha Haugnes and Jennifer L. Russell, "Don't Box Me In: Rubrics for Artists and Designers," *To Improve the Academy* 35, no. 2 (2016): 264.

39. Haugnes and Russell, "Don't Box Me In," 264.

40. Marian Shaffner, *Fostering Creativity Using Real Clients: Creativity* (San Francisco, Elixr Merlot, 2009), http://pachyderm.cdl.edu/elixr-stories/fostering-creativity/.

41. Maryellen Weimer, *Inspired College Teaching* (San Francisco: Jossey-Bass, 2010), 75.

42. Terry Doyle, *Helping Students Learn in a Learner-Centered Environment: A Guide to Facilitating Learning In Higher Education* (Sterling, VA: Stylus Publishing, 2008).

43. Maryellen Weimer, *Inspired College Teaching* (San Francisco: Jossey-Bass, 2010), 88.

44. Philip Stark, "What Exactly Do Student Evaluations Measure?," *The Berkeley Blog,* October 24, 2013, http://blogs.berkeley.edu/2013/10/21/what-exactly-do-student-evaluations-measure/.